DESIGNING
YOUR OWN
COMPUTER GAMES

DESIGNING YOUR OWN COMPUTER G·A·M·E·S

David Ritchie

QUILL
New York

Library of Congress Catalog Card Number: 84-61112

ISBN: 0-688-03928-6

Printed in the United States of America

First Quill Edition

1 2 3 4 5 6 7 8 9 10

BOOK DESIGN BY PATRICE FODERO

To Raisin and Snowflake, good friends and great pets

ACKNOWLEDGMENTS

Many persons have helped with making this book. Chief among them are Nick Bakalar and Carol Mann, whose patience and good advice were invaluable.

CONTENTS

A NOTE ON MATH

We will be using math extensively in this book, so this is a good place to review the various mathematical operations. The ones below should be familiar to you already:

$$+ \quad \text{Addition}$$
$$- \quad \text{Subtraction}$$
$$/ \quad \text{Division}$$
$$* \quad \text{Multiplication}$$
$$= \quad \text{Equal to}$$
$$< > \quad \text{Not equal to}$$

Most home computer systems use a double asterisk (**) to stand for exponentiation, or raising a number to a given power; thus:

$$2**3 = 2*2*2 = 8$$

Some systems, however, may use another symbol, such as a vertical arrow (↑), to show exponentiation, so that:

$$2**3 = 2 \uparrow 3$$

Check your system's programming manual, and make the appropriate corrections to the programs in this book if necessary.

Another programming technique you must understand is the use of parentheses—( )—in equations. The computer treats anything between parentheses as a single expression. So the positioning of parentheses can have a great effect on the outcome of a calculation.

Here are two examples. In the first equation there are no parentheses, and the computer simply carries out one operation after the other in sequence:

$$
\begin{aligned}
X &= 3*4 - 6 + 2/4 \\
&= 12 - 6 + 2/4 \\
&= 6 + 2/4 \\
&= 8/4 \\
&= 2
\end{aligned}
$$

Put two pairs of parentheses into that string of numbers and operations, however, and you get quite a different result:

$$
\begin{aligned}
X &= 3*(4-6) + (2/4) \\
&= 3*(-2) + (0.5) \\
&= -6 + 0.5 \\
&= -5.5
\end{aligned}
$$

Parentheses, then, are powerful tools for organizing the math in your programs. Use them carefully!

You may find it necessary at times to "nestle" one set of parentheses inside another, like this:

$$
\begin{aligned}
X &= (5*(4*(3*2))) \\
&= (5*(4*6)) \\
&= (5*24) \\
&= 120
\end{aligned}
$$

Just make sure that each parenthesis on the left side is balanced by another on the right. Otherwise there will be a "hole" in your equation caused by a missing parenthesis, and the program will not run. There should always be an even number of parentheses in your equation.

As you get into more advanced game programming—especially graphics—you will have to use trigonometric functions such as SIN, COS, etc. In this book we touch only briefly on trigonometry, but it is a good idea to look up the trigonometric functions in your programming manual and practice using them, because on many occasions they come in handy to represent something in picture form.

DESIGNING
YOUR OWN
COMPUTER GAMES

CHAPTER 1

You Can Do It!

SOME DAYS ARE PERFECT, and this was one of them. A cool wind was blowing in off San Francisco Bay, the Berkeley hills rose green and inviting in the distance, and the waters sparkled in spring sunshine as a friend and I sat down for a lunch of fish and chips on the waterfront.

It's hard to think troubled thoughts in a setting like that. So it was surprising when my friend said, "It's a shame."

"What is?" I asked.

He munched a mouthful of fried potatoes for a few seconds, then replied, "You know that computer I was working on when you came into the store today?"

I nodded. He was a skilled electronics technician and had been repairing an expensive home computer system when I stopped by his store a few minutes earlier.

"I was checking it out by playing a videogame on it," he went on, "when something occurred to me. It was junk."

"The computer?"

"No, the game. It was so dumb and shoddy, it was pathetic."

"Well, it's not supposed to be *War and Peace*," I pointed out. "Computer games are supposed to be fun, not great works of art."

"Of course they are," he said, stabbing energetically at his fish. "But how much fun are they, really? You chase a spaceship or a snake or something around the screen for a little while. You try to gobble it up, or chop it to bits, or shoot it down.

"After an hour or so, it gets a little boring. The spaceship can only make so many moves, and the computer can only throw so many aliens and other obstacles at you. The longer you play, the more you realize it's just a dumb, simpleminded game that keeps its novelty interest for only a couple of hours. Then it gets stale, and you put it away and hardly ever use it again. Now, how much do you think you've spent for that little bit of recreation?"

"Well," I said, "the game costs thirty dollars. . . ."

"It can go up to fifty."

"All right, fifty dollars. You need a computer system to play it on. . . ."

"Two hundred to a thousand."

"Joysticks and paddles . . ."

"Another hundred dollars or so."

"So we're talking," I concluded, "about an investment of several hundred dollars at least."

"At the very least," my friend replied. "That's why I say it's a shame." He took a bite of his fish, then continued:

"It's not just the cost of these games that bothers me. If people were getting their money's worth from most of the games, it would be fine. But they're not.

"They're shelling out hard-earned dollars to buy games of which maybe eighty percent are pure junk. The games move some little critters around on the screen, and that's about all. So if you buy one of these turkeys, you've spent maybe a whole day's pay to play somebody else's dumb and boring little electronic fantasy. Zap the aliens, catch the monster, avoid the sniper. Ho-hum. Would you pay thirty dollars for that, let alone several hundred?"

"No," I answered, "but there are arcades."

"More dumb games," my companion said. "And those quarters add up fast. You can spend twenty dollars a week in one of those places if you're not careful."

"Of course," I said, "people can design their own games. . . ."

This is how books are born.

On a visit to New York some weeks later, I had lunch with an editor and said to him, "Want to see a book on how to design computer games?"

"Sounds interesting," he said. "What are the advantages of designing your own computer games?"

Quite a few, as it turns out:

1. *You save money.* There's no need to shell out a handful of tens—or even a handful of quarters—to play someone else's game when you can design your own, at home, for virtually no expense.

2. *It's fun.* Designing computer games is like playing basketball, or painting pictures, or working crossword puzzles. It's a pleasure. It occupies your mind wonderfully and provides a perfect antidote to boredom. And since the most effective education is the kind you enjoy . . .

3. *You learn a lot.* Are you ignorant of what goes on inside your home computer? You won't be after programming a few games of your own. Designing your own computer games probably is the best way to learn computer programming, because the pleasure of gaming makes the learning much less tedious.

4. *You can make money.* That got your attention, didn't it? If you can come up with an entertaining computer game, then you may be able to sell it to a company for a handsome piece of change. Or if you're the entrepreneurial type, you may be able to market it yourself and make even more money off the deal.

Unfortunately, some fears and misconceptions have kept many folks away from this enjoyable and profitable hobby. Here are a few of them:

- *I'm not a genius.* Very few of us are. So it's lucky that you need not be a tremendous intellect to design computer games successfully. One well-known designer of my acquaintance is anything but a mastermind. In fact, he once scored a below-normal 85 on a standardized IQ test. Yet he creates entertaining games that have been collected in book form and have earned him quite a lot of money. Meanwhile, many of his more brilliant friends from high school and college are trying to parlay their Ph.D.s into jobs driving taxis.

  So don't be deterred by the myth that only geniuses can design computer games. If that were the case, there would be very few games around.

- *I can't handle complex programming.* You might be astonished to see how simple many popular computer games really are on the programming level. Recently I saw the printout for a popular arcade-style game. The program filled only a couple of pages. Nothing about it was very complicated. All the commands in it were simple BASIC, the same computer language we will be using in this book. Everything in the program was within the comprehension of the average person. All you needed to understand the program were elementary reading skills and the ability to count to ten without making an error. Dissecting that program to see how it worked took only about an hour.

  This book will show you how games are structured, and with that knowledge you ought to be able to write programs of your own with very little trouble.

- *I'm scared I'll make a mistake.* So what if you do? No one's going to shoot you for misplacing a PRINT statement here and there, or typing in 10 where you meant to put 100. The worst that can happen is that your program won't run. Then all you need do is go back and see where you made your error. The computer won't laugh at you or slap you on the wrist. On the contrary, your computer will be enormously patient with your efforts and will allow you all the time you need to get your program entered and running properly.

- *It's too much work.* If that's your attitude, then chances are you'll never get very far as a game programmer—or as anything else, for that matter. To succeed in the field of computer game design, you will have to put in a lot of time and effort at the keyboard—more time and effort, in fact, than you may think reasonable at times.

There will be moments when your head aches, your eyes burn from staring overlong at the screen, your shoulders hurt from long hours hunching over a keyboard . . . and the deleted, censored, unprintable program still will not run. You will be sorely tempted to heave the computer out the window, because all you have to show for hours of struggle is a little message such as "OUT OF DATA" or "SYNTAX ERROR."

Scream if you like, or toss a cushion across the room, but please resist the urge to punch out your computer. Unless your computer is defective, the fault is not with the machine. You're just doing something wrong. Get up, walk around, have a soda or whatever, and come back a little later for another try.

When the work load and frustration seem too much to bear, just recall the soothing words of Thomas Alva Edison, who said that "success is ninety-nine percent perspiration and one percent inspiration."

Also, computer game programming, like every other field of human activity, is governed by Murphy's three famous laws:

Nothing is as easy as it looks.
Everything takes longer than it should.
If anything can go wrong, it will . . .
at the worst possible moment.

But even the struggle can be fun. It's exhilarating to pit yourself against an especially intractable game program and see if you can make the machine produce your dream on screen.

Would that there were some easy prescription, some simple formula that could make you a master programmer overnight. But there isn't. You'll just have to get in there and practice. As Euclid said once to his king, there is no royal road to knowledge, and that advice applies to game programming as well as to anything else.

If you get discouraged, there's a man you should remember. His name was Francisco José de Goya y Lucientes. We know him simply as Goya.

Goya was one of the most famous painters of the nineteenth century, and in the realm of art there was very little he couldn't do.

Goya mastered just about every form of graphic art. At the library you can see the etchings he made of bullfights. Even in black and white, the images are so vivid that you can practically see the bright colors of the bullring . . . and the blood in the arena. With a well-selected line Goya makes you hear the thump of hooves on sand and feel the vibration of the stands beneath you as the crowd jumps and roars.

Then look at Goya's portraits. One of the most famous is his self-portrait as a sick old man being tended by a physician. This is quite a different picture from those of the bullfights. The colors are muted, the outlines soft and blurred. No lively motion catches your eye. Still, the painting holds your attention because it looks so quietly but overwhelming real. You can almost hear the rasp of an ill man's breath and smell the odor of medication in the room. The picture is every bit as riveting as Goya's bullfight scenes but in a completely different way.

And then there is Goya's well-known painting of a street carnival. What a contrast with the previous pictures! Here Goya painted his vision in wild colors, with all the abandon of a Leroy Nieman canvas: a single flowing wave of vivid hues and brilliantly suggested froms surging forward like a Waikiki breaker. Goya is said to have painted this masterpiece with a spoon. Even working with that crude tool, he was able to create one of the greatest images of revelry ever captured in a picture.

How could this one man execute three such marvelous yet greatly dissimilar works of art?

Goya could do it because he knew his craft inside out—and he knew it that well because he practiced it endlessly.

Every day he drew, or etched, or painted. From every picture he learned a lesson, and he applied that lesson to improving his art. Near the end of his life he drew a cartoon of himself as an old man hobbling along on a pair of canes. The caption read, "I'm still learning."

That's how devoted Goya was to his art. If you can muster even 5 percent of his industry and patience, then you may become the next master designer of computer games, and connoisseurs in the next century may value your work as highly as collectors value Goya's today.

Only you can decide whether computer games are worth the time and effort you will have to put into them. You may be encouraged to know, however, that the time is ripe for a breakthrough in game design and concepts—and perhaps you will be the one who achieves it.

Here's the situation: As of this writing (late 1983), videogame makers are worried about a slump in sales. People aren't buying shoot-'em-up adventures for their home game systems anymore. Only recently one manufacturer had to hire a bulldozer to bury thousands of unsold game cartridges that were cluttering up warehouse shelves.

The depressed videogame market has put hundreds of videogame company employees out of work, and more than a few executives are said to be running around their offices screaming, in Little Caesar fashion, "Mother o' mercy! Is this the end??!"

No, it is not the end . . . at least not the end of computer games. It looks as if the home computer is here to stay; and as long as people own home computers, people will be playing games on them. We are a game-playing species, so there always will be a market for good, entertaining games, whichever medium we use to play them.

Fortunately, we appear to be seeing the end of the flashy, noisy, mindless videogame that caused such a revolution in tastes and recreational habits during the late 1970s and early 1980s. Just as earlier crazes, such as the hula hoop, peaked and then declined after a few years, videogames seem to be on a slow ride downhill.

Why? For one thing, they've lost their novelty value.

There was a time when it was the height of something to man a joystick and blast multicolored alien blobs out of the blue on your home screen. But it appears those days are gone, for the newness of videogames is gone too. Buyers today are looking for something different. They want fresh games, novel challenges—and they are looking to you to supply them.

Also, many videogames have been, to put it charitably, unoriginal. Consumers would buy what they thought was a variety of home videogames only to find, after sampling several of them, that they merely had been playing the same game with different graphics. Someone had substituted a new set of characters for an old bunch on some previously existing game and then marketed the camouflaged old war-horse as a totally new production.

Then there's what you might call the Harold Hill syndrome. You remember Professor Harold Hill. He was the charismatic con artist portrayed by Robert Preston in that grand old movie *The Music Man*. In one scene Hill tries to whip the residents of a small Iowa town into a moral frenzy by warning them of the perils posed by a pool table in their community. "Ya got trouble!" he announces, then proceeds to tell the Iowans how that infamous game may lead their young'uns into sin and corruption. The answer, Hill warns, is to ban the demonic game.

Professor Hill's ghost is still abroad these days, only his target is no longer pool but rather its modern equivalent: arcade videogames. Communities from New England to California have tried, in the interest of curbing delinquency, to have coin-operated arcade games banned so that kids will not be exposed to the "unwholesome" influence of those little bleeping blobs of light.

More often than not, the critics of computer games have been playing a much older game called Find the Scapegoat. It's easier for mothers and fathers to blame computer games for their children's shortcomings than to consider that they, the "ideal parents," might have gone wrong somewhere, or that their darling offspring might have botched things up on their own. In previous generations the scapegoat was the comic book, the jitterbug, or rock 'n' roll. Today it's the videogame.

How much has the campaign against videogames done to cause their decline? That's hard to say, but the war on videogame "addiction" has undoubtedly had a negative effect on game sales and most likely will do so for some time to come.

So why should would-be game designers be optimistic? They are looking at a possible road to riches.

If arcade-style games are on the way out, then something will be coming along soon to replace them. What it will be, no one can foresee exactly, for the future of computer games has so far been extremely hard to predict. (Could anyone looking at the crude space-war games of a decade ago have envisioned, back then, the games of interstellar combat we play today?)

The wave of the near future may be story games, or nongraphic puzzles, or something else entirely.

It might be a game that *you* devise.

The point is, you have an opportunity, in a rapidly changing computer-game market, to introduce games that might become the crazes of the late 1980s and beyond.

Doesn't that inspire you to master the art of game programming?

WHAT YOU'LL NEED

1. A *computer.* Naturally. Better make it one of the top-selling systems. No one will look twice at the games you devise if they're written for the Unknown Mark III.

2. A *monitor.* Depending on your system, you may need a color TV set or other such monitor, or a plain old black-and-white portable may do.

3. *A tape recorder or disc drive.* You'll need to store your work in electronic form for future reference.

4. *A printer.* There are plenty of occasions when you will want a printout of your work to ponder at the dinner table, send through the mail, or review in the study hall.

5. *Two books.* One is a good general-purpose BASIC programming guide. The other is a programming manual for your particular system, preferably including a section on machine language—a topic we'll address in detail later.

6. *Patience.* Oodles of it.

You should also keep up with at least a few of the magazines and newsletters devoted to computer games. They frequently print game programs you can enter on your machine and dissect, line by line, to see how they work.

You probably have most of these items already. The rest you can acquire new or used. Even at bargain-basement prices, however, we are talking here about an investment of at least several hundred dollars and possibly more than a thousand.

This means that if you want to become proficient at computer game programming, you will have to sink some cash into the quest along with your blood, toil, tears, and sweat.

Has this chapter scared you off yet?

No? Then you are made of stern stuff and just may turn out to be the next master game designer. Even if you're not bound for the top, game design can provide you with hours of pleasure and maybe a little spending money on the side.

But all programmers have to follow certain fundamental rules of game design. We'll look at those now.

CHAPTER 2

What's in a Game?

QUICK! WHAT'S A GAME?

If someone asked you that question, you would probably answer "football," or something of the sort. And you would be wrong.

Football, baseball, and the like are specific games. But what is a game, in the general sense of the word? What makes up a game, and how do you organize one?

Think about those questions for a while and you will realize that games are more subtle and complicated than you probably ever imagined.

First things first. How do you define a game?

One good definition is "organized play." It makes a clear distinction between games and play, for not all play is a game. Games are special forms of play, guided by particular rules toward specific goals.

Here are some illustrations. Kicking a ball along in front of you, as you walk, is play. Kicking a ball in football or soccer is part of a game. Tossing a rubber ball against the side of a building, then catching the ball on the rebound, is play. Handball—an organized version of such play—is a game.

What makes the difference in each case is the way the play is organized and directed. Here are the things that set games apart from mere play:

1. *Goals.* Game play is aimed toward some goal or objective—that is, something you are playing to get. It may be prize money, a trophy, or just the satisfaction of getting a winning hand of cards, but in every case there is a goal to be attained.

2. *Rules.* Rules help to organize the play in games. The rules state what you may and may not do as you go for the goal. No hitting below the belt. No going offside. Don't touch the ball with your hands. Three strikes and you're out. Without rules like these, games would be mere anarchic play.

3. *Scores.* When playing a game, you need a quantitative measure of how the play is progressing. If you play alone, then you need to know how close you are to your goal. If you play against someone, then you need to know who is ahead, and by how much. Here's where scores come in. They serve as markers in the course of a game and as indicators for a goal. Indeed, a certain score is often itself the goal.

So in summary:
Goals are what you aim for in a game.
Rules tell you how to get there.
Scores reveal how far along you are.
These, however, are not the only ingredients of games. Another essential ingredient is *Challenge.*

No game is interesting if it's too easy. You need a difficult obstacle to overcome, and preferably several of them, on the way to your goal.

In team sports, such as football, the obstacle is the opposing team. On the way to the opponents' goal line, you have to run an obstacle course of players who are doing their best to keep you from getting there. You may also have to contend with a muddy and slippery field, incompetent teammates, and blind referees. And just when you think you've beaten them all, out of nowhere lurches a three-hundred-pound linebacker who rolls right over you and ends your sprint to victory.

All successful computer games have interesting challenges built into them. The protagonist may have to make his or her way past prehistoric monsters, hostile troops, unfriendly ghosts, or Henry VIII waving a headsman's ax . . . but the challenge is what makes the game.

By contrast, the least successful games have the least challenge. Without naming names, let me tell you the story of a less than gifted game designer whose game fell flat for this very reason.

A CAUTIONARY TALE

Once upon a time a game designer decided to try his hand at an arcade-style game.

He started out with a traditional theme: cops and robbers. Fine. That theme has inspired some highly entertaining computer games.

Next, he animated a robber and set him loose in a maze. If the crook got through the maze and evaded the cop who pursued him, then the bad guy was home free. So far, so good.

But things went downhill from there . . . because the cop wasn't bound by the maze! He was free to leap over all the obstacles in his path and swoop down on the thief like a hawk on a rabbit. The robber, on the other hand, was restricted to within the maze's walls, which made him less maneuverable than the cop.

Where was the challenge in that? If the cop had been forced to find his way through the maze in pursuit of the crook, then the game might have been great fun. The cop and his quarry would have been evenly matched, and the challenge facing them both—the maze—would have made the game one of luck and skill.

Absence of challenge, however, made the game thoroughly dull and consequently a failure. The magazines panned it. "Don't waste cash on this turkey," they warned readers. The designer's star descended fast, and his game sank into the oblivion it deserved.

Moral: Thou shalt challenge the player . . . or else.

There are countless ways to build challenges into your game. They may come from other players, from the field of play, or from the sheer blind chance that deals you an unexpected hand.

That brings us to yet another key component of computer games: *Unpredictability.*

You can't make the game too predictable, or else players will get bored. And you can't afford to let that happen. It's the worst error a game designer can commit.

Players will put up with just about any flaw in a computer game as long as the game holds their interest. You probably have seen a few games that had infantile animation but still were fun to play.

When the play gets tedious, however, the fun is gone and you might as well dump the disc or cartridge in the trash, because no one will play that game again.

You can afford to tease, vex, and even outrage your audience, but you must never bore them. This is one line of work where yawns are fatal.

So keep 'em guessing. Throw in unexpected events. Have the floor drop out of a room, or a bomb explode, or someone walk through a doorway firing a rifle.

However you do it, add an element of the improbable and unpredictable to your games and you'll avoid putting players to sleep. There are lots of occasions where a simple surprise can cover a multitude of shortcomings in a game. The players won't see the game's defects so clearly because they will be wondering what may happen next.

We'll soon learn more about probability and game design. For now, let's say that a simple but effective programming trick can introduce a delightfully devilish element of unpredictability into your games and give the players hours of entertainment.

But all this advice will do you no good unless you have a decent idea for a game to start with.

Fortunately, ideas for games are everywhere. You can simulate already existing games such as baseball, shot put, or pole vaulting.

If you find those too mundane, then you are free to "improve" on them by inserting variations that could never occur in the real world. What would happen, for example, if football had to be played on a saddle-shaped field instead of a flat one? What if hockey players had to perform in zero gravity and in three dimensions instead of on a flat rink in a normal one-gravity field? What would baseball players do if someone literally kept stealing bases?

In the fantasy world of computer games, anything can happen. So let your imagination run free. See what becomes of your favorite sport when you model it in a computer program and then start tinkering with the variables. You can even dream up totally new games, with rules and goals straight out of your own imagination. Who knows? You might create a new national pastime!

Sometimes the origins of computer games are as interesting as the games themselves. One of the games in this book was inspired by a struggle to put a flea collar on a very large and uncooperative cat. Another, MOSCOW, has its roots in an old Walt Kelly comic book. (See "The Man from Suffern on the Steppes" in Kelly's anthology *Ten Ever-Lovin' Blue-Eyed Years with Pogo*.)

History games often are good bets. The War Between the States has inspired some memorable computer games. So have the Napoleonic and Hellenic wars and the global conflicts of our own century. It's great fun to sabotage historical legends, such as those of Charlemagne, or Paul Revere's ride (the true story of which isn't the one you read in your grade-school history books), or Richard III (who wasn't nearly as evil as Shakespeare made him out to be).

Ah, Shakespeare! His plays are full of good material for computer games. There's one game that pits Shakespeare against several of his spookiest characters—including the three witches from Macbeth, and the ghost of Hamlet's feather—in the dimly lit corridors of Elsinore Castle. (Will the Bard manage to evade his pursuers and get out of the castle in time to pick up a manuscript from Francis Bacon? Wait and see!)

BEWARE OF TOCs

What are TOCs? They are among the most dangerous pitfalls that await the unwary game designer—tired old clichés!

Swords and sorcery. Space battles. Cute little critters doing cute pointless things. These are just a few examples of TOCs—themes that have been worked and overworked until the mere mention of them is enough to send customers running out of software stores, screaming and holding their noses.

Whatever you do, avoid the TOCs. Climb Pike's Peak in your swim fins if you have to, but under no circumstances court a TOC.

How do you spot the dreaded TOC? Easy. Go into the nearest store that has a large selection of computer games and look at the packages. If the illustrations show more than ten of something—spaceships, dragons, wizards, or whatever—then chances are it's been a TOC for years. If it shows up four or five times, then it's well on the way to TOCdom.

And if a certain theme or idea or character doesn't appear at all, then it may be fresh and unhackneyed enough to make a good new game!

An idea, however, is only the nucleus of a game. Much work remains to be done.

CHAPTER 3

Down
to BASICs

WHEN YOU DESIGN and program a computer game, you will have to overcome three barriers: the "brain barrier," the "language barrier," and the "documentation barrier." Let's look at them one by one.

Most of the games we play involve a special kind of thinking. Scientists call it "left-brain activity," for it generally takes place in the left half, or hemisphere, of the brain.

The left side of your brain is the "hard headed" part of your thinking equipment. This is the cool, calculating, number-juggling part of your brain and mind—the mental domain where logic resides. On this side of the brain you try to bring order out of chaos, try to analyze things to see how they work.

By contrast, the right side of the brain is the home of our "mushier" thought processes: intuition, creativity, and so forth. Have you ever had a sudden but inexplicable burst of insight, or a hunch that seemed totally illogical but later turned out to be correct? Then you have experienced the right side of your brain at work.

These two halves of your mind are so different that sometimes they have trouble communicating. An invisible barrier— the "brain barrier"—seems to separate them.

One of your jobs as a computer game desiger will be to break down the brain barrier. You will have to get the right and left sides of your brain working smoothly together.

You see, only on the right side of your brain can you dream up interesting ideas for games, and only on the left side can you translate those ideas into the coldly logical language of computers. Once you get the two halves of your brain working together, you should be able to turn out some good games and have a lot of fun doing it. Don't worry; overcoming the brain barrier isn't hard. If you can work a crossword puzzle, then you probably can hop over the brain barrier with no trouble at all.

How will you know when you've overcome that hurdle? Probably when something like the following happens:

You will be walking down a street and see some children playing baseball in a nearby lot. The pitcher throws the ball, the batter hits it, the ball flies up in a high graceful arc toward center field—and in your mind's eye you see not merely a fly ball but also a dot on a display screen, following a mathematically defined curve with a sine function in it. You will be able to make a good guess as to which equation the curve should follow and what sequence of commands you will need to reproduce that fly ball in a computer game. You will see the game as a logiclly ordered series of commands, subroutines, and data. And this whole train of thought will occupy only a couple of seconds.

That's when you will know the brain barrier is down. You will start seeing everyday events in terms of computer games. The fall of a leaf or the flight of a bird will bring a program listing to your mind.

None of these events will lose their beauty or pleasure. You will simply see them—perhaps for the first time—in left-brain and right-brain fashion at once, just as you would if converting them into computer images.

One game designer I know remembers the moment he first realized he had overcome the brain barrier: "I was watching *Dirty Harry* on TV. You know the scene where Harry is pointing his gun at the punk but can't remember whether he's fired five shots or six? Immediately I thought, 'X = RND *6.' That's how a programmer would describe the moment Harry pulls the trigger." Down went the brain barrier. That particular game designer now is living in New England and making good money from his work.

The brain barrier is only a little problem compared to the language barrier. Before you can succeed as a game designer and programmer you will have to learn a whole new way of expressing yourself, for computers "talk" in ways much different from human speech.

Ordinary human language is not suited for communicating with computers, for they represent the ultimate in left-brain activity. Computers are rigidly logical. Right-brain thinking means nothing to them. Moreover, computers are so stupid that they can do only one thing at a time. They have to complete one operation, then proceed to the next, and then the next, and so forth until the whole job is done.

You, though, have a much more sophisticated "computer"—your brain—which can handle many different operations at the same time. So you probably are unused to thinking in "computerese" and sometimes have trouble putting your thoughts into computer languages.

The most widely used language in home computer systems is BASIC (Beginners' All-purpose Symbolic Instruction Code). Developed at Dartmouth College in the 1960s as a learning aid for novice programmers, BASIC is a simple and easily learned language, with many expressions taken straight from everyday English: PRINT, PLOT, NEXT, etc.

The problem with BASIC is that it is not always "spoken" the same way. There are many different variations on BASIC—a different one, in fact, for almost every home computer system on the market.

The situation is much as George Bernard Shaw put it when he described the English and the Americans as two peoples separated by a common language. One make of computer may have trouble handling any BASIC "dialect" except its own. A BASIC program that runs perfectly on one home computer system may be useless on another system because they use two different variants of the language.

Why this Babel of BASIC derivatives? Business competition is one reason. The computer makers want you to use their products and no one else's—so they invent their own versions of BASIC to make sure you are restricted to using only their software with their computers. You have to make changes in their programs if you want them to run on a different system.

Fortunately, these changes usually are minor. Translating one BASIC "dialect" into another is often no more complicated than adding punctuation here and subtracting a word there. That little equation we mentioned several paragraphs back, $X = RND *$ 6, might show up in other BASIC variants as LET $X = (RND *$ $6) + 1$, or $X = RND * 6 + 1$.

Here's another illustration. Suppose you are displaying some patterns on the screen and want to put an asterisk in the upper left-hand corner. One system's BASIC allows you simply to write in the coordinates of the asterisk following a PRINT statement, and the asterisk will appear at that spot on the screen.

You type in:

10 PRINT AT 3,3;"*"

The computer will print an asterisk in the upper left-hand portion of the screen, three lines down from the top and three spaces to the right of the left-hand margin.

But another system may lack this capability. In that case you will have to use another programming technique to get that asterisk in place. Try writing in the following lines:

10 PRINT
20 PRINT
30 PRINT TAB 3;"*"

This accomplishes the same thing as programming PRINT AT (3,3); "*". The first two PRINT statements tell the computer to print nothing on those initial two lines, starting at the top of the screen and moving down. On the third line, represented by line 30 in the program, PRINT TAB 3; "*" tells the computer to print out whatever lies between those quotation marks (which themselves do not appear on screen) three spaces to the right of the left-hand edge of the picture.

The result is the same in both cases. You get an asterisk printed just where you want it. The only difference is that one kind of BASIC allows you to do the job more straightforwardly than the other.

If you are far enough along with your computer to be interested in designing games for it, then you ought to be thoroughly familiar with its brand of BASIC already. So you probably won't have much difficulty converting the programs here into a form your computer can handle.

What if you *do* have trouble? That's a sign you're unprepared. Go back and study your system's programming manual.

KNOW YOUR SYSTEM'S PROGRAMMING LANGUAGE

You wouldn't go to live in a foreign country without knowing the language, so apply the same principle to your programming. Don't attempt to design and program computer games until you know your system's programming language inside and out and can translate other systems' BASIC variants into one your system can use. That little bit of preparation will save you a lot of frustration and wasted time later on!

We've saved perhaps the biggest barrier for last: the documentation barrier. "Documentation" is the five-dollar word for all the printed material that is supposed to tell you how to use your system. "Documentation" also is something of a swear word among home computer users, because so much documentation is garbage.

If you have a home computer and have spent a few hours trying to make sense of the instruction manual and programming guide, you probably have seen how awful most documentation is. The authors appear to have flunked English 101. They can't communicate in plain language. Their instructions are poorly organized, and they simply ignore many questions that novice programmers are likely to ask, such as, "How do you get this machine to count from 1 to 10 on its own?"

In fact, much documentation is so bad that authors have had to write instruction manuals to explain the already existing instruction manuals!

Maybe someday computer manufacturers will come to grips with the documentation problem and spend as much time and effort putting together instructions as they spend putting together their computers. Meanwhile, you will have to make the best of what documentation you have and search out manuals that explain your system and its programming most clearly.

CHAPTER 4

One Step
at a Time

RIGHT NOW visions of great games probably are dancing through your head, and you're eager to get started. That's wonderful.

But before you sit down at the computer and start typing in commands and data, do a little preliminary work on your game—for a good beginning will make final success more likely.

A computer game, like any other work of art, doesn't simply leap into existence fully formed. It is built one step at a time, from a basic plan or outline that gives the game its structure. Just as a painter sketches figures in chalk on the canvas before painting them, you will have to "rough in" an outline of your game to make programming easier.

How you do this is up to you. Some game designers insist on using formal "flow charts"—those big diagrams full of rectangles, diamonds, rhomboids, and hexagons filled with words ("DISPLAY INTRODUCTION," "INPUT NAME," or whatever) and tied together with lines and arrows. A flow chart shows you in pictorial form everything that happens in a program from start to finish.

Such a diagram can come in handy, especially if you are working on a very long and complicated program. The flow chart allows you simply to follow a line with your finger to see which parts of the program are doing what to one another.

Making flow charts is a complicated subject and far beyond the scope of this book. Fortunately, the games we will examine here are simple enough that flow charts will not be needed to understand them. (For detailed instructions on how to draw up flow charts, see the recommended readings.)

We can make do with a plain verbal account of what is going on in the programs. And if you are designing and programming relatively elementary games, then a few short paragraphs of instructions should serve you perfectly well to structure your work.

Here is the method used on the games in his book:

1. *Summarize* the goal of the game in a few words. ("This game will simulate a soccer match.")

2. *Describe* the major steps to be followed in programming the game. ("Draw the playing field. Animate the players and the ball. Program in rules and scoring system.")

3. *Break down* those major steps into their smaller component procedures. ("To draw the playing field, draw two horizontal lines extending all the way across the top and bottom of the screen. . . .")

4. *Program* these verbal descriptions into BASIC.

5. *Run* the program when it's finished.

6. *Debug* the program if it doesn't run as you wish.

Sounds easy, doesn't it? Well, it is—after you've programmed a few dozen games successfully. You probably have a lot of work ahead, however, before you reach that level of proficiency.

Until then, here are a few suggestions that will make your work easier:

1. *Keep it simple.* This advice applies on two different levels: structure and programming.

There's a danger that you will get bewitched by the intricacies of computer gaming and dream up games so complex that no one can play them but you. Whatever else you do, don't make that mistake!

Always remember that the most enduring and entertaining games are, generally speaking, also the simple ones. They have easily understood goals and only a few fundamental rules.

You ought to be able to state the goal of your game in ten words or less: "Knock the other guy out." Or "Get the ball to the opposite end zone." Or "First player to get a hundred points wins."

There should be as few rules as possible. Try to keep them down to half a dozen or so, and certainly no more than a player can count on his or her fingers. (The human mind really does have trouble keeping track of any set of things greater than ten. Ask someone to name all the gifts presented in the song "The Twelve Days of Christmas"!)

Simplicity should reign on the programming level as well. Never use two commands or statements when one will do. This policy will make the program easier for you to write, and for users to enter into their computers.

This doesn't mean your should make your games simpleminded . . . just simple. Too many games fall flat because they violate the maxim that "Simple pleasures are the best."

2. *Take your time.* Many novice game designers set to work with berserk energy. They start work at 8:00 A.M. and expect to have a finished arcade-style game program done and recorded before noon.

    They are almost always disappointed, for it takes a long time to get a good game program drawn up and running.

    You will need days or even weeks to get your games programmed and polished to an acceptable degree. This is partly because it takes time to plan and then execute a successful game program, and partly because old Murphy is looking over your shoulder as you work, making sure things go wrong and delay you. The more complex and sophisticated your programs become, the more opportunity Murphy has to cause mischief.

So if you think you will need an hour to finish a certain subroutine, better allow two hours, just to keep Murphy happy.

And if you have to spend an extra evening sweeping the last of the wee unexpected bugs out of your work, who cares? The world won't come to an end if you take a little extra time on a program. On the contrary, your game probably will turn out to be much improved for that added time and effort. Better a few ripe works than a lot of green and raw ones!

3. *Take occasional breaks.* Professional writers have a saying, "Tired writing makes tired reading." How true. If you sit down at a typewriter keyboard—or a computer—in a weary state of mind, then your fatigue will show up in your writing or your programming, and the results will be rotten.

Computer game programmers have it even rougher than writers do. The writer merely has to translate his or her thoughts into words that a reader's mind can grasp, whereas the programmer has the much more daunting task of converting his or her ideas into BASIC or some other language conceived for the nonhuman "mind" of the electronic computer.

It may take hours or even days to express in BASIC a train of thought that could be put forth in everyday language within seconds, because thinking in computer language— even a relatively simple and forgiving computer language such as BASIC—can make a four-minute mile look easy by comparison.

That's why many programmers tend to develop facial tics and jump at sudden noises after a few hours at their labors. Programming is hard work!

So avoid long, straight stretches of programming. Take a short break every hour or two. Get up and leave the computer alone for a while. It's not going anywhere.

Spend a few minutes doing something to take your mind off the computer program. Stand on your head, read a newspaper, or have a cup of coffee. Do anything that will carry your thoughts away from all those PRINTs and TABs and PLOTs momentarily.

You will come back to work refreshed—and likely to do a much better job of programming.

4. *Read programs backward.* No, don't try to read them from the rear side of your printout! Instead, start at the end of your program and read in reverse order toward the beginning. Along the way you may see things you miss when reading the program in the normal sequence.

5. *Let it cool when done.* When you take a hot cherry pie out of the oven, do you bite into the pie right then? No. You put the pie aside for a while to cool, and you go back to it later.

    Do the same thing with your programs. When you've finished a game program, record it. Then leave it alone for a few days. When you look at the program again, you probably will see a lot of things—including possible improvements—that you overlooked before in the heat of creative thinking.

6. *Keep several copies.* Programs stored on tape or disc are terribly fragile. They can be destroyed by heat, cold, magnetic fields, programming errors, or an accidental spill of coffee.

    If that happens, it's more than a waste of time and effort. It's also the most horrible feeling you can experience. One designer I know saw a beautiful program of his wiped out completely. He looked pale and broken in spirit for days afterward. "It's like losing a child," he said in a hollow tone of voice.

    There is an easy way to avoid this tragedy. Simply keep at least two copies of each computer game you work on, updating the copies as the game progresses. That way, if your master copy is lost or ruined, you will have backup copies.

Keep the copies in a safe place—preferably a stout wooden box lined with lead foil and covered with a tight lid—to ensure that nothing, from smoke to magnetism, can reach the discs or tapes and undo your labors. One of these secure storage containers costs only a few dollars and can either be built from scrap wood or purchased at a store or through the mail.

That's all for the preliminaries. Next we will take apart some sample programs to see how they work.

Nearly all the BASIC expressions in these programs ought to be familiar to you already. Some are explained here in detail, in the context of a program. For short explanations of others, check "A Quick BASIC Glossary" at the back of this book. (More extensive information can be found in your system's programming manual.)

CHAPTER 5

RND-Om
Thoughts

A FEW PAGES back we mentioned the role of chance in games. Game play is more fun if it owes something to luck, and inserting an element of chance is easy—with the RND, or random number, function.

RND activates a random number generator inside your computer. It probably is more accurate to call it a "pseudorandom number generator," because in most home computer systems RND tells the computer to select from a string of several hundred random numbers that already were selected and stored in the machine's memory. The computer then will pick numbers at random from that list, one at a time, as it is called on to do so.

You never know which number is going to turn up next. For example, suppose you told the computer to pick numbers at random from 0 to 100. The instruction might be written out as follows:

$$X = INT (RND * 100)$$

This equation tells the computer to pick a series of "integers"—that is, whole numbers—such as the following:

10
4
22
48
9
78
22
43
89
1
1
7

You can use RND to excellent effect in games by linking game play to the random number selection process. If, say, X = 7, a screaming pink Valkyrie thunders onto the football field and spears a fullback. Or if X = 10, the ball turns out to be a time bomb and explodes in the pass receiver's face. You get the idea.

Incidentally, it's wrong to assume that each random number picked by the computer will be different from the number before. It's possible (though not very likely) that you will get a run of the same number now and then: 1111111111111, perhaps.

That's roughly equivalent to hitting the jackpot at a slot machine on your first quarter. It doesn't happen often, but it does happen. So expect the unexpected when you put RND into your games. Your games will improve, and players will enjoy them more.

Here are some exercises to get you used to using RND. First let's use RND to simulate a roll of dice:

```
10 PRINT "BABY NEEDS A NEW PAIR OF
SHOES."
20 A = INT (RND * 6)
30 B = INT (RND * 6)
```

```
40 PRINT A ; B
50 GOTO 10
```

A sample run of that program will look like this:

```
BABY NEEDS A NEW PAIR OF SHOES.
2 3
BABY NEEDS A NEW PAIR OF SHOES.
4 3
BABY NEEDS A NEW PAIR OF SHOES.
2 2
```

. . . and so on, until you stop the run.

Now let's practice on a more sophisticated program called MOSCOW.

The action in MOSCOW takes place during a session of the Supreme Soviet. In theory the Supreme Soviet is the equivalent of our U.S. Senate and House of Representatives rolled into one. In practice, however, the Supreme Soviet has very little power. Its job is merely to provide a rubber stamp for preapproved Kremlin policies and to give the several hundred delegates an excuse to have fun in the big city.

Let's suppose you are the delegate from Lower Kulakistan. One night you have several vodkas too many and get suckered into a game of Russian roulette.

Here's how the game goes: There are two players. Your opponent in this game is the delegate from Blechski, one Comrade Nastikoff. Your weapon is a revolver, and your target is your own head.

Put one bullet in the revolver and leave the other five chambers empty. Then spin the chambers around so that there is no way to tell whether the next shot will be a dud or a live round of ammunition.

Place the gun to your temple and pull the trigger.

If the gun goes off, the game is over, and you lose. Otherwise you hand the gun over to Nastikoff, and he repeats the procedure. The first player to happen upon the bullet loses. They really know how to have fun over there.

Here is a harmless computer simulation of this game. All the while you read this program, keep in mind several questions:

- What is the best way to do this on your computer?
- How does this game fit in with the guidelines mentioned earlier in this book?
- Are there other ways to carry out the operations in this program? Would a different set of commands do just as well?

05 REM "MOSCOW"

Always start a program with REM followed by the name of the game in quotation marks. REM allows the computer to locate the game again when you call it up from storage on tape or disc.

```
10 PRINT "IS TIME TO PLAY MOSCOW"
20 PRINT "ROULETTE, COMRADE."
30 PRINT
40 PRINT "PERFECT WAY TO (HEH, HEH)"
50 PRINT "KILL TIME ON LONG WINTER
NIGHT."
60 PRINT
70 PRINT "REVOLVER HAS SIX CHAMBERS"
80 PRINT "BUT ONLY ONE BULLET."
90 PRINT
100 PRINT "HERE IS HOPING IT WILL
NOT"
110 PRINT "HAVE YOUR NAME ON IT."
120 PRINT
130 PAUSE 250
```

Line 130 is a simple way of pacing the action of a game. PAUSE 250 tells the computer to stop and count, at its own speed, from 1 to 250. That works out to roughly four or five seconds. Your system may require another programming trick— perhaps something like FOR X = 1 TO 250: NEXT X. Check your programming manual for details.

```
140 PRINT "READY? GOOD LUCK."
150 PAUSE 250
160 CLR
```

Line 160 clears the screen.

```
170 PAUSE 250
180 PRINT
190 PRINT "YOU GET FIRST SHOT."
191 PAUSE 250
192 PRINT "(LUCKY YOU.)"
193 PAUSE 250
194 CLR
195 A = 1
```

Wait a minute . . . where did that A = 1 come from?

It's an important part of the program, because it will help to determine whose turn is next. (You wouldn't want to miss a chance to blow your brains out, would you?) A little later we'll see how this A value fits into the program's overall structure.

```
200 IF A = 1 THEN GOSUB 300
```

You will see much more of GOSUB, because it will be one of your most useful tools in computer game design. GOSUB allows you to drop what you are doing, do something else for a while, then return and pick up again where you left off. It's like putting a call on hold and taking another telephone call on a second line.

We have already established in line 195 that A = 1. This number means that you get the first shot, as promised in line 190.

Now line 200 is about to shuttle you off to a subroutine, starting with line 300, that will give you that initial shot. You may want to glance ahead to line 300 to see just what the shooting (literally!) is all about.

```
210 IF A = 2 THEN GOSUB 400
220 IF A = 3 THEN GOSUB 300
230 IF A = 4 THEN GOSUB 400
240 IF A = 5 THEN GOSUB 300
250 IF A = 6 THEN GOSUB 400
```

See what's happening here? Whenever A is an odd number, the program gives you a turn (GOSUB 300). Evens mean it's the turn of your opponent, who gets his or her shot starting with line 400.

```
300 X = INT (RND * 6)
```

Ah—here's our old friend RND again. This time RND substitutes for the revolver and selects at random a number from 1 to 6, corresponding to one of the chambers of the gun. The number picked in line 300 is the chamber on which the hammer comes down.

The big question here is: Which chamber holds the bullet?

```
310 IF X = 1 THEN GOTO 500
```

There's our bullet, in chamber one. If the hammer falls on that one, then GOTO 500 will refer the computer to a later part of the program that describes your grisly death.

```
320 IF X <> 1, THEN GOSUB 600
```

This is the start of your "lucky day" GOSUB . . . RETURN loop.

If the hammer comes down on an empty chamber (that is, an X value other than 1), then you get sent along to line 600 and saved from an untimely end.

330 RETURN

Don't forget that RETURN! It completes the GOSUB . . . RETURN loop begun in line 200.

400 X = INT (RND * 6)

Line 400 is identical to line 300 because your opponent is repeating here the same sequence of events you went through in the 300s. The only difference is that depending on which number is picked in line 400, we advance to line 700 or line 800.

```
410 IF X = 1 THEN GOTO 700
420 IF X <> 1 THEN GOSUB 800
430 RETURN
```

Now to "kill you off":

```
500 CLR
510 PRINT
520 PRINT TAB 12, "***BLAM***"
530 PAUSE 250
540 CLR
550 PRINT "YOU LOSE, COMRADE."
560 STOP
```

Note that STOP at the end of the 500s. STOP has to be there, because you're dead!

If you're lucky and the gun goes "CLICK" instead of "BLAM" on your turn, then Nastikoff gets a try:

```
600 CLR
610 PRINT TAB 12, "CLICK"
620 PAUSE 250
630 PRINT
640 PRINT "SO FAR SO GOOD."
650 PRINT "NOW HAND OVER GUN."
660 PAUSE 250
670 A = A + 1
```

Aha—the return of variable A.

We first met A back in line 195, remember, in connection with whose turn it is. Now A reappears, to transfer the gun to your opponent.

Each time, the value of A increases by 1, making an even number odd (meaning it's your turn) or vice versa (your opponent's turn).

```
680 CLR
690 RETURN
```

Again, don't forget RETURN . . . you need it to balance the GOSUB in line 320.

Here's where Nastikoff gets it:

```
700 CLR
705 PRINT "WILL LUCK BE WITH"
710 PRINT "NASTIKOFF?"
715 PAUSE 250
720 PRINT
730 PAUSE 250
```

```
735 PRINT
740 PRINT TAB 12, "***BLAM***"
745 PAUSE 250
746 CLR
747 PRINT TAB 12, "THUD"
750 PAUSE 250
751 CLR
755 PRINT "HOO BOY, YOU LUCKY."
756 PRINT "YOU SURVIVE ..."
757 PAUSE 250
758 PRINT
759 PRINT "AT LEAST UNTIL NEXT"
760 PRINT "POLITBURO MEETING."
770 PRINT
775 PAUSE 250
780 PRINT "AND NOW A MOMENT'S"
785 PRINT "SILENCE FOR OUR DEAR"
790 PRINT "DEPARTED COMRADE."
795 PAUSE 500
796 STOP
```

The next few lines show how Nastikoff cheats death and how PAUSE can be used to build suspense.

```
800 CLR
805 PRINT "NASTIKOFF TAKES GUN ..."
810 PAUSE 250
815 PRINT
820 PRINT "SQUEEZES THE TRIGGER ..."
825 PRINT
830 PAUSE 250
```

```
835 PRINT "AND ..."
840 PRINT
845 PAUSE 500
850 PRINT TAB 12, "CLICK"
855 PRINT
860 PAUSE 250
865 PRINT "WHEW"
870 PRINT "YOUR TURN AGAIN."
875 PAUSE 250
880 A = A + 1
885 CLR
890 RETURN
```

Make any appropriate modifications to this program, enter it on your computer, and run it. If you have done your work correctly, then a typical run should go like this:

```
IS TIME TO PLAY MOSCOW
ROULETTE, COMRADE.

PERFECT WAY TO (HEH, HEH)
KILL TIME ON LONG WINTER NIGHT.

REVOLVER HAS SIX CHAMBERS
BUT ONLY ONE BULLET.

HERE IS HOPING IT WILL NOT
HAVE YOUR NAME ON IT.

READY? GOOD LUCK.

YOU GET FIRST SHOT.
(LUCKY YOU.)
```

```
CLICK

SO FAR SO GOOD.
NOW HAND OVER GUN.
WILL LUCK BE WITH
NASTIKOFF?

        ***BLAM***

          THUD

HOO BOY, YOU LUCKY.

YOU SURVIVE . . .

AT LEAST UNTIL NEXT
POLITBURO MEETING.

AND NOW A MOMENT'S
SILENCE FOR OUR DEAR
DEPARTED COMRADE.
```

This is, of course, the very roughest skeleton of a game program. You can do much better with time and practice.

All kinds of interesting variations of this game are possible. You might modify it for more than two players. What would that do to the handling of the A variable?

For laughs, you might insert a phony gun that shoots borscht instead of bullets. That way a loser might be humiliated without getting killed. (It would also make the game more realistic. No one expects a player who just got shot to rise from the dead and start to play again.)

And just to keep things interesting, try to arrange another RND so that the proceedings are interrupted, every dozen games or so, by the secret police—who break up the game and warn that it is illegal to kill yourself without the government's permission!

Notice that something was missing from this game: a formal scoring system. There was no need for one, because every game ought to end 1–0, with the loser dead on the floor. Other games, however, let players live to see their final scores. How would you arrange a scoring system for a nonlethal game of chance?

Right: a B variable!

Insert a line at the appropriate place in the program, to the effect that B equals $B+X$ or $B-X$, the X in this case being the number of points you stand to win or lose.

Now you are about to see the A variable in action again, but in a less dangerous kind of gambling.

Here the scene is the fictional Monte Cello casino, and you are about to play a highly modified version of ordinary roulette.

You start the game with $10,000 and may bet any portion of that sum, up to the whole bundle, on any given spin of the wheel. If you lose, the amount of your bet is subtracted from your available funds. If you win, however, you receive ten times the amount of your wager! Then you are free either to keep on betting, or to quit while you're ahead.

As we dissect this program, watch the arithmetic in it closely and you will learn a lot about scoring procedures.

```
05 REM "MONTE CELLO"
06 A = 10000
07 PRINT "WELCOME TO MONTE CELLO."
08 PRINT
09 PRINT "YOU NOW HAVE $"; A
10 PRINT
20 PRINT "HOW MUCH WILL YOU BET?"
30 INPUT B
```

INPUT B lets you enter the amount you want to bet. Be sure to hit the RETURN key after typing in the number.

```
40 PRINT "YOU BET $"; B
50 PRINT
```

```
60 PRINT "NOW PICK A NUMBER FROM 1
TO 36."
70 INPUT C
```

INPUT C is the number you want to bet on.

```
80 PRINT "YOU CHOOSE NUMBER "; C
```

Make sure you leave a space between the second pair of quote marks and the last letter of the last word inside them. If you don't, then there will be no space between the word and number on the screen.

```
90 IF C< 1 THEN GOTO 1000
100 IF C> 36 THEN GOTO 1000
```

You are allowed to pick only from numbers 1 through 36. If you accidentally pick 0 or a number greater than 36, lines 90 and 100 will refer you to a later line that informs you that your choice is unacceptable.

```
110 PRINT "THE WHEEL SPINS ..."
120 PRINT
```

Let's leave the wheel spinning for a moment and examine the line that determines where the ball will come to rest.

```
130 D=INT (RND * 36)
```

Just a little sleight-of-RND.

```
140 PRINT "BALL LANDED ON "; D
150 IF C = D THEN GOTO 200
```

You won!

```
160 IF C <> D THEN GOTO 300
```

You lost.

```
200 CLR
210 PRINT "CONGRATULATIONS. YOU
WIN!"; (B * 10)
220 A = (A - B) + (B * 10)
```

In line 210 we tally up your winnings, and in line 220 we add them to what remains of your initial $10,000 (that is, A−B) after placing this bet.

You can use similar arithmetic to add points to a score after a goal, or to subtract points for a foul.

```
225 GOTO 500
```

Lines 500 through 590 register your decision to quit or keep playing.

With luck, A will keep growing steadily. You are more likely to lose on any given bet, however, and lines 300 through 325 show the fate of the unlucky at this game:

```
300 PRINT "SORRY, THAT WAS NOT"
310 PRINT "YOUR LUCKY NUMBER."
320 A = A - B
325 GOTO 500
```

Here in the 500s block you are about to make the acquaintance of a useful programming tool: INKEY$.

```
500 PRINT "DO YOU WANT TO CONTINUE?"
510 PRINT
530 PRINT "TYPE Y FOR YES, N FOR
NO."
```

```
540 S$ = INKEY$
550 IF S$ = ""THEN GOTO 540
560 IF S$ = "Y" THEN GOTO 09
570 IF S$ <> "Y" THEN GOTO 580
580 IF S$ = "N" THEN STOP
590 IF S$ <> "N" THEN GOTO 540
```

INKEY$ is called a "string variable." (For more information on this, see "A Quick BASIC Glossary" at the end of this book.) It is a great time-saver, for INKEY$ allows you to punch in a character—in this case, Y or N—without having to hit the RETURN key, as you do when using INPUT.

But there's a trick to using INKEY$. If you are a little slow in entering something, the computer will make a choice for you—whether it's the right choice or not! To keep that from happening, use the safeguard seen in line 550.

If nothing is entered (that's what " " means), then the computer will just keep going back to line 540 and waiting for you to punch something in. Lines 560 through 590 register your entry of Y or N. And if you press the wrong key by accident, don't fret. These lines are programmed so that if you hit anything *but* one of those two keys, the computer returns to line 540 and keeps waiting for an acceptable entry.

Punch in Y, and line 560 will shuttle you back to line 09, which will print out the adjusted total for you.

Here is a sample run of the game:

```
WELCOME TO MONTE CELLO.
YOU NOW HAVE $10000.
HOW MUCH WILL YOU BET?
YOU BET $1000.
NOW PICK A NUMBER FROM 1 TO 36.
YOU CHOOSE NUMBER 5.
THE WHEEL SPINS ...
```

```
BALL LANDED ON 23.
SORRY, THAT WAS NOT
YOUR LUCKY NUMBER.
DO YOU WANT TO CONTINUE?
YOU NOW HAVE $9000.
HOW MUCH WILL YOU BET?
YOU BET $100.
NOW PICK A NUMBER FROM 1 TO 36.
YOU CHOOSE NUMBER 8.
THE WHEEL SPINS ...
BALL LANDED ON 8.
CONGRATULATIONS. YOU WIN $1000.
YOU NOW HAVE $9900.
DO YOU WANT TO CONTINUE?
```

The real-life game of roulette is much more complicated than this exercise. For one thing, a genuine roulette wheel has more than thirty-six slots. There are also two "house numbers," 0 and 00, which serve to give the house a theoretically unbeatable advantage.

When you place a bet, you do so on the assumption that you have a one-in-thirty-six chance of winning. That's about 0.028, or 2.8 percent.

But in fact you have only a one-in-thirty-eight chance—0.026, or 2.6 percent—because of those two extra numbers, which the house pretends are not there at all. Yet even though they theoretically don't exist, you lose if the ball lands on one of them!

Thanks to those house numbers, the casino has an advantage of 7.7 percent:

$$(0.028/0.026) - 1 = 1.077 - 1 = 0.077$$

That advantage guarantees that the house will make a profit in the long run, even if a gambler gets lucky now and then and wins a million or two.

How might you insert those house numbers into the game? (Hint: if D>36 . . . then what?)

The games we've seen so far have steered clear of graphics. It's nice to enliven your games with pictures, but computer graphics can be terribly complicated to program. So let's sneak up on them and look next at a game illustrated with very simple graphics that will help prepare you to tackle something tougher.

CHAPTER 6

Roll
the Bones

EARLIER WE SIMULATED, in a very elementary way, the roll of a pair of dice. Let's look at that program again:

```
10 PRINT "BABY NEEDS A NEW PAIR OF
SHOES."
20 A = INT (RND*6)
30 B = INT (RND * 6)
40 PRINT A ; B
50 GOTO 10
```

That program printed out the two numbers generated by lines 20 and 30 on each roll.

This wasn't a very dramatic game—unless you happen to enjoy watching a pair of numbers pop up on the screen time and again. Why don't we enliven it with some graphics?

At the mention of the word "graphics," some novice programmers get the cold sweats and start looking around the room for the nearest exit. Graphics? Those hideously complicated things full of mysterious commands and machine-language values? Eek!

Don't panic just yet. Some computer graphics are very complicated, while others are very simple. But all computer graphics operate on the same principle: They translate programs into pictures. So devising graphics is merely a matter of writing a proper program; and as we mentioned earlier, nothing in programming home computer games is beyond the capabilities of a patient and determined person.

With those words of encouragement, let's look at the "canvas" on which computer graphics are "painted."

A computer screen is divided into vertical and horizontal coordinates. Each spot on the screen has its own pair of coordinates. On the system used to develop these games, 3,3 means three lines down from the top and three lines from the left-hand margin of the screen. So the first number in this pair is the vertical coordinate, and the second number is the horizontal coordinate.

When our imaginary die comes to rest after a throw, one of its faces points straight up. On the face may be any one of six numbers, from 1 to 6. So on a given throw, you might get something like:

```
       0
        0
         0
```

Or:

```
    0       0
        0
    0       0
```

Those graphics are about as simple as you can get, so it shouldn't be too much trouble to write a program to reproduce them. And it isn't. Watch.

We won't need line 40 anymore, because we are going to print out designs instead of mere numbers. To make things easier, we might well get rid of lines 10, 30, and 50 as well. We won't need to return to line 10, and it will simplify matters if we have to deal with only one graphic rather than two. That leaves:

```
20 A = INT (RND * 6)
```

Line 20 "decides" which number the die will show. This number will control printing a graphic like those shown above.

If A = 1, then the program will produce a graphic showing a single dot. If A = 2, two dots. If A = 3, three dots. And so forth.

How do we tie line 20 to its appropriate graphics? It's easy to do with an IF . . . THEN loop.

The IF . . . THEN loop comes in handy on countless occasions because it lets you have several different plans of action ready to be implemented as the occasion demands. IF such-and-such happens, THEN you do so-and-so. That's the purpose of the IF . . . THEN loop.

In line 20, there are six possibilities, since RND may come up with any number from 1 through 6. And in each case the computer will have to print out a different graphic. So:

```
40 IF A = 1 THEN GOTO 100
50 IF A = 2 THEN GOTO 200
60 IF A = 3 THEN GOTO 300
70 IF A = 4 THEN GOTO 400
80 IF A = 5 THEN GOTO 500
90 IF A = 6 THEN GOTO 600
```

If the computer selects the number 1, then line 40 tells the computer to look ahead to line 100 and print out a single-dot graphic.

```
100 PRINT AT 9,9; "0"
110 STOP
```

That's all there is to it! The computer prints out a single dot, nine lines down from the top and nine lines over from the left margin.

What if your computer doesn't have that kind of "shorthand" for positioning the dot on the screen? Fear not; you only have to add a few short lines to the program.

Insert several PRINT statements to move your dot down to the desired level; thus:

```
100 PRINT
101 PRINT
102 PRINT
103 PRINT
104 PRINT
105 PRINT
106 PRINT
107 PRINT
108 PRINT TAB 9; "0"
```

You may not have to write a new line for each of those PRINTs. Your system may allow you to "scrunch" the program by putting a colon (:) between them so you can fit them all on a single line; thus:

```
100 PRINT:PRINT:PRINT:PRINT:
PRINT:PRINT:PRINT:PRINT
```

Don't forget to put in STOP in line 110! If you don't, then the computer will just keep on going to line 200 and everything after it—and print *all* the sets of dots on the screen.

```
200 PRINT AT 9,8; "0 0"
210 STOP
```

That's what happens when A = 2.

When A = 3, you have two choices, depending on how industrious you feel. You can either print the dots all on one line and save a little effort . . .

```
300 PRINT AT 9,7; "0 0 0"
310 STOP
```

. . . or you can arrange the dots on a diagonal, as they actually appear on dice:

```
300 PRINT AT 8,8; "0"
301 PRINT AT 9,9; "0"
302 PRINT AT 10,10: "0"
310 STOP
```

Note how those two numbers just after AT determine the positions of the dots. The pattern is centered on location 9,9—the same location that the single dot had in line 100. To add another dot, just above and to the left, subtract one from the first nine (that elevates the dot) and one from the second nine (moving the dot back horizontally one space). Next, to print out a dot just to the right and down, add one to the first nine and one to the second nine to make the coordinates 10,10. The rest of the program you can follow for yourself:

```
400 PRINT AT 8,8; "0 0"
410 PRINT AT 10,8; "0 0"
420 STOP
500 PRINT AT 8,8; "0 0"
510 PRINT AT 9,9; "0"
510 PRINT AT 10,8; "0 0"
520 STOP
600 PRINT AT 8,8; "0 0 0"
```

```
610 PRINT AT 10,8; "0 0 0"
620 STOP
```

There you have it! When printed out, your dice graphics ought to look like this:

```
            0       0 0     0       0     0 0 0
  0     0 0     0                       0
            0       0 0     0       0     0 0 0
```

That wasn't too hard, was it? If you did everything correctly, then you saw how easily you can turn a program into patterns on a screen. All you need to know is where a symbol is going and what kind of programming will put it there.

Now let's move on to slightly more advanced graphics, and a slightly spooky game that will teach you much about tying graphics to game play.

CHAPTER 7

GLOMP!

HERE'S A GOOD GAME for Halloween parties.

Look at the map of southern New Jersey and you will see a vast area of swampy, wooded land known as the Pine Barrens. This underdeveloped corner of the Garden State has fascinated and mystified outsiders for centuries, and out of it have come all kinds of myths and legends.

For instance, there's the legend of the "air tune," the faint melody that one sometimes can perceive there but that remains forever just outside the range of hearing. So the story goes, anyway.

Don't spend too much time listening for the air tune if you are traveling alone on foot through the Pine Barrens, however, because a supernatural power is said to lurk there, too: the infamous Jersey Devil!

From time to time, over a span of more than two hundred years, the residents of the Pine Barrens and surrounding territory have reported seeing and hearing a bizarre creature that appeared to be made up of parts from several different species.

Here is how one alleged eyewitness described the beast as seen in flight over a river in 1909:

Its head resembled that of a ram with curled horns. It had long, thin wings and short legs. It made a mournful and awful call, a combination of a squawk and whistle.

That fiendish-looking beast came to be known as the Jersey Devil. It caused mass panic in the Pine Barrens just prior to the First World War. Several thousand persons in more than twenty different towns claimed to have fled the Devil as it squawked, whistled, and puffed its way through the swamps and woodlands. The apparition left behind a smell like that of dead fish or rotting potatoes.

When word swept through the Pine Barrens that the Jersey Devil was aproaching, schools and stores closed, and everyone retreated behind locked doors and shuttered windows. No one except that one "eyewitness" quoted earlier actually reported seeing the Devil, but clues to the monster's passage were everywhere. Frightened Jerseyites claimed to have found the Devil's footprints all over the ground. In some places the tracks ran for a few feet along the surface, then mysteriously ended, as if the animal that made them had suddenly taken flight.

Other reports said that shortly after the Devil scare the bodies of several dogs were found mauled and ripped apart by the claws of some great and vicious creature. And from scattered corners of the Pine Barrens, word seeped out about strange steaming ponds and bogs that had supposedly been heated to boiling by the Jersey Devil's fiery breath.

Little was heard of the Jersey Devil for the next several decades. Possibly the New Jersey folk were too concerned about human monsters such as Hitler and Mussolini to worry about a legendary one.

But then the Jersey Devil reportedly staged a comeback in Gibbstown, New Jersey, in the early 1950s. Two boys said they had seen the Devil's terrifying face peering at them through a window. "Devil mania" rippled through the Pine Barrens once again for a while, making journalist I. F. Stone's description of that decade—the "haunted fifties"—seem literally true for New Jersey.

The Devil's most recent appearance was in the winter of 1979. Several youngsters skating on an icy pond reportedly sniffed a foul odor of decay and went to find the source of the smell. Suddenly they found themselves looking into two huge and ghastly eyes staring down from the head of a specter seven feet tall! The kids retreated—unfortunately without any evidence to support their story.

Is the Jersey Devil merely a myth, or does something unspeakable really inhabit the depths of rural New Jersey, munching on stray animals and occasionally scaring the wits out of passersby?

There is no solid evidence that the Jersey Devil exists—except in the minds of those who believe in it.

Yet let's not consign the Jersey Devil to mythology for good. Sometimes tall tales turn out to be attached to living, flesh-and-blood animals. Gorillas, for instance, were considered to be mere fantasies until a live gorilla was captured and brought out of the jungle for scientists to study.

So perhaps we ought to keep an open mind about the Jersey Devil until its existence is either proven or disproven beyond a doubt.

Meanwhile, if you live in or near the Pine Barrens, it might be best to keep your pets indoors at night—just in case.

Here's a game based on the legend of the Jersey Devil. Again, as you follow along, keep in mind how you can translate this game into a form suitable for your own home computer.

```
05 REM "DEVIL"
10 PRINT TAB 10, "THE JERSEY DEVIL"
20 PRINT
30 PRINT "THIS GAME IS BASED ON THE"
40 PRINT "LEGEND OF THE JERSEY
DEVIL."
50 PRINT "YOU ARE SLOGGING YOUR WAY
THRU"
```

```
60 PRINT "A SMALL PART OF THE NEW
JERSEY"
70 PRINT "PINE BARRENS. THERE IS NO
ROAD."
80 PRINT "THE SWAMPY GROUND PREVENTS
YOU"
90 PRINT "FROM RUNNING. YOU MUST
TAKE"
100 PRINT "A LONG AND WINDING ROUTE"
110 PRINT "TO REACH THE NEAREST
SHELTER."
120 PRINT "ALONG THE WAY YOU WILL
HAVE"
130 PRINT "TO AVOID THE JERSEY
DEVIL,"
140 PRINT "WHO CAN POP UP ANYWHERE,"
150 PRINT "AT ANY TIME, AND DEVOUR
YOU."
160 PRINT "ONLY ONE PLACE IS SAFE--"
170 PRINT "A CABIN IN THE WOODS."
180 PRINT "SEE IF YOU CAN BEAT THE
DEVIL."
190 PRINT "(TYPE C TO CONTINUE.)"
200 PRINT
210 PAUSE 60
220 LET M$ = INKEY$
230 IF M$ = " " THEN GOTO 220
240 IF M$ = "C" THEN GOTO 290
250 IF M$ <> "C" THEN GOTO 220
260 CLR
```

Clear screen for action!

```
295 PRINT AT 1,1:"0"
```

That 0 in line 295 stands for your goal, the cabin in the woods. This pair of coordinates will make the 0 appear in the upper left corner of the screen.

So far, so good. Next, draw a maze through which you will have to pick your way, step by soggy step, to reach the cabin. We'll make this maze very simple so that the programming will be easy to follow. Later you can go back and make the maze more complicated if you wish.

```
300 FOR Y = 3 TO 11 STEP 8
```

Here the variable Y stands for the vertical axis on the screen. When Y=1, you are at the top of the screen, and as Y increases, you work your way down. Line 300 tells the computer to count from 3 to 11 on the Y axis and skip eight spaces between each count. Since $3+8=11$, the computer will mark off only lines 3 and 11 from the top of the screen.

```
310 GOSUB 400
```

Having counted off those two points on the vertical axis, the computer will now skip ahead to a subroutine that prints something at those locations. Before you jump ahead to line 400 and check, though, better look at the following few lines to see what happens just before then.

```
320 FOR Y = 7 TO 15 STEP 8
330 GOSUB 500
340 GOSUB 600
```

See what we're doing? Lines 320 and 330 carry out the same functions as the preceding two lines did, only they're marking off lines 7 and 15 from the top and telling a subroutine to print something there. Don't worry about line 600 yet; we'll get there soon enough. Go on to line 400 and note how we start drawing the maze.

```
400 FOR X = 1 TO 27
410 PRINT AT X,Y;"-"
```

Now we're getting somewhere!

Here X stands for the horizontal axis on the screen. Line 400 informs the computer that something is going to happen in spaces 1 through 27 on the horizontal axis. Then line 410 tells the computer what to do in those spacs: Print out a hyphen (-).

Lines 300 and 310 aleady have set the vertical coordinates for these horizontal lines, so the result will be two horizontal lines of hyphens, each line twenty-seven spaces long, at locations three and eleven spaces from the top of the screen.

Nothing says you have to print out a hyphen, by the way. If you prefer, then by all means use an asterisk (*) or a colon (:) or whatever instead.

The next two lines are *very* important. Look at them carefully.

```
420 NEXT X
430 NEXT Y
```

Why are these lines so significant? Each is part of a FOR . . . NEXT loop.

Lines 420 and 430 make sure that every time the computer prints out a hyphen at coordinates Y and X, the computer then will go on to the next pair of listed coordinates until the whole line is done.

Remember: The computer is so stupid it cannot "think" ahead even to the next step unless you remind it to do so. That's why NEXT X and NEXT Y are essential to this program.

```
440 RETURN
```

And, of course, RETURN takes us back to the point where we left off before this subroutine began. The computer now looks over its shoulder, so to speak, and "sees," from line 320, that the next subroutine starts with line 500. If you understand what went on in lines 400 through 440, you will have no trouble with lines 500 through 540.

```
500 FOR X = 3 TO 29
510 PRINT AT X,Y;"-"
520 NEXT X
530 NEXT Y
540 RETURN
```

This is the previous subroutine all over again, but with a slight difference. Lines 500 through 540 print out another pair of horizontal lines, but these are slightly staggered with respect to the other two.

That completes the part of the program that draws the maze. If you have done your part of the job correctly, you ought to see on your screen a pattern like this:

0

Well, it's not the Hampton Court Garden, but it will do for now. You must move a symbol through this maze from lower right to upper left, one step at a time; thus:

```
0 . . . . . . . . . . . . . . . . . . . . . . . . . .
                                                    .
  — — — — — — — — — — — — — — — — — — — — — — —  .
                                                    .
  . . . . . . . . . . . . . . . . . . . . . . . . . .
  .
  .    — — — — — — — — — — — — — — — — — — — — — — —
  .
  . . . . . . . . . . . . . . . . . . . . . . . . .
                                                    .
  — — — — — — — — — — — — — — — — — — — — —    .
                                                    .
  . . . . . . . . . . . . . . . . . . . . . . . . .
  .
  .    — — — — — — — — — — — — — — — — — — — —
  .
  . . . . . . . . . . . . . . . . . . . . . . . . .
```

You are *not* allowed to touch any of the lines in the maze. *Strange things* happen to people who bump into the lines, as we will see in a moment.

What about the star of our show, the Jersey Devil? Rest assured, he'll be here. He doesn't take his terrifying physical form in this game, but that makes him all the more dangerous—for you can't see him crouching near you. He's lurking out there, silent and invisible, waiting for you to blunder across him.

The Devil can pop up in your path anywhere, at any time, except in the cabin. Only there are you safe!

Fortunately for you, even the Jersey Devil can't be everywhere at once. So there's a chance you will escape his clutches. In fact, you and the Devil will be about evenly matched in this game once the program is finished and running. Let's proceed.

```
600 A = 18
610 B = 30
620 PRINT AT A,B;"X"
```

"X" marks the location of our intrepid traveler. To avoid confusion with the vertical and horizontal axis figure used already, we use variable A to stand for his vertical position and B for his horizontal position.

How will the computer know when Mr. or Ms. X reaches shelter and safety? Easy. It's just a matter of a few IFs:

```
623 IF A = 1 THEN GOTO 625
624 IF A <> 1 THEN GOTO 630
625 IF B = 1 THEN GOTO 1000
626 IF B <> 1 THEN GOTO 630
```

See what's happening?

Line 623 says that if the traveler winds up on the same horizontal line with the cabin—that is, on the line at the top of the screen, where $Y = 1$—then he or she might be at the cabin itself. There's only one way to find out, and that's to see if the traveler's horizontal coordinate equals that of the cabin—namely, 1.

So line 623 refers us down to line 625. If the traveler really has reached the cabin, and $B = 1$, then you've evaded the Jersey Devil, and a little celebration is in order (see line 1000).

But if you're not on that uppermost level, then A will be unequal to 1, and line 624 will pass you on along to line 630. The same thing happens if you are on the same level as the cabin but you haven't quite reached it yet (that is, $A = 1$ but $B <> 1$). You still have some plodding to do, and you have to move on to line 630:

```
630 PRINT AT A - 1, B;" "
640 PRINT AT A + 1, B;" "
641 PRINT AT A, B - 1;" "
642 PRINT AT A, B + 1;" "
```

Lines 630 through 642 allow the traveler to cover his or her tracks so the Jersey Devil can't spot them. No matter which direction the traveler moves on the screen—up, down, right, or left—these lines will remove the X printed at the traveler's previous location.

To see how we move the X around, look at lines 650 through 675:

```
650 IF INKEY$ = "L" THEN B = B - 1
```

If you press down the L key, the computer moves the X one space to the left by subtracting one from the X's horizontal coordinate.

```
660 IF INKEY$ = "R" THEN B = B + 1
```

To move to the right, line 660 adds one to the horizontal coordinate.

```
670 IF INKEY$ = "U" THEN A = A - 1
```

Line 670 moves the X one space upward by subtracting one from its vertical coordinate . . .

```
675 IF INKEY$ = "D" THEN A = A + 1
```

. . . while line 675 does just the opposite.

```
680 GOTO 700
```

Study this next section carefully, for it's a bit complicated.

```
681 IF A = 3 THEN GOTO 689
682 IF A <> 3 THEN GOTO 683
683 IF A = 7 THEN GOTO 692
684 IF A <> 7 THEN GOTO 685
685 IF A = 11 THEN GOTO 689
```

```
686 IF A <> 11 THEN GOTO
    687
687 IF A = 15 THEN GOTO 692
688 IF A <> 15 THEN GOTO
    620
689 IF B <= 27 THEN GOTO
    2000
690 IF B > 27 THEN GOTO 620
691 IF B < 30 THEN GOTO
    2000
692 IF B > 29 THEN GOTO 620
693 IF B <= 29 THEN GOTO
    694
694 IF B >= 3 THEN GOTO
    2000
695 IF B < 3 THEN GOTO 620
```

Lines 681 through 695 are something like a "traffic control system" for action on the screen. This part of the program tells the computer whether you've bumped into the maze lines.

Line 681 says if X lands on the top line (A = 3) of the maze (which has a little recess at the far right of the line to let the X pass through that level), then it's time to check line 689 of the program. Lines 689 to 690 tell the computer whether you've bumped into the maze (spaces 1 through 27, horizontally).

If you hit the wall of the maze, then B will be less than or equal to 27, and line 689 will refer you to line 2000, which tells you that you went astray, you fumble-footed oaf, and you will have to start the game over! (See? Strange things *do* happen to people who bump into those horizontal lines!)

What if A, your X's vertical coordinate, is unequal to 3? In that case line 682 tells the computer to glance down the rest of the list to check to see if you've collided with any other lines.

If you get all the way down to line 688 safely, then you're clean and can make another move. You may notice that if you merely brush past one of the horizontal lines of hyphens—that is, within a single space on either side—your "track covering" system, described in lines 630 through 642, erases a hyphen in the line. Don't fret about that. You are penalized only if your X itself collides with a horizontal line.

Now we're going to see a "devil generator":

```
700 F = INT (240 * RND)
705 IF F <> 100 THEN GOTO 681
710 IF F = 100 THEN GOTO 715
```

Line 700 tells the computer to pick an integer (that is, a whole number, such as 1, 2, 3, and so on) between 0 and 240.

Why 240? We said earlier that you and the Jersey Devil would be about evenly matched in this game. That means the Devil stands roughly a 50 percent chance of glomping you on any given run of the game. These F values are what give you a fighting chance.

Here's how: From start to finish, the traveler will move approximately 120 spaces on the screen. That's 120 chances for the Jersey Devil to pop up and glomp the X.

If the F value chosen in line 700 is unequal to 100, then the traveler is safe (at least for that move). If the random number generator in the computer comes up with F = 100, however, the traveler gets glomped (see line 715)!

Had we set the random number generator to pick a number only up to 120—the approximate number of moves from start to finish—then the Jersey Devil would have an advantage. Over the long run line 700 would come up with F = 100 in almost every game, and the X would get glomped with monotonous regularity.

But what if we give the computer a bigger "pool" of numbers to pick from? In that case the chance of getting glomped diminishes because there is less likelihood that the computer will pick *your* number.

Confusing? Then think of these figures in terms of a school of fish.

If you are fish number 100 in a school of 120, and if a hungry barracuda darts through the school 120 times, trying to snap up a fish on each pass, then you are virtually sure to get swallowed.

If you are fish number 100 in a school of 240, however, then you will stand only half as great a chance of getting eaten. The school is twice as big as it was before, and therefore your chance of survival goes up from nearly 0 to about 50 percent.

This is why we use 240 * RND in line 700; 240 is twice 120. So in any given game the computer stands only a 50 percent chance of picking your unlucky number between start and finish.

If you play a hundred times, chances are you will win about half of them and get glomped roughly every other time. You and the Jersey Devil will be evenly matched.

Now go back and check out lines 681 through 695. They're still waiting for you. Thereafter we'll just be mopping up.

What follows is the "glomping" sequence:

```
715 PRINT AT A, B; "OH, NO"
720 PAUSE 200
725 PRINT AT A, B; "          "
```

Line 725 erases your exclamation without clearing the entire screen, by printing blank spaces in place of the letters.

```
730 PAUSE 200
735 PRINT AT A,B; "***GLOMP***"
740 PAUSE 200
745 PRINT AT A,B; "          "
750 PAUSE 200
755 PAUSE AT A,B; "(BURP)"
760 PAUSE 200
765 PAUSE AT A,B; "          "
```

```
770 PAUSE 200
780 CLR
781 PRINT "OOPS ... BETTER LUCK"
782 PRINT "NEXT TIME."
783 PAUSE 300
784 CLR
785 GOTO 1080
```

Now here's the victory sequence. Go ahead. Pat yourself on the back.

```
1000 CLR
1010 PRINT "WHOOPEE"
1020 PAUSE 200
1030 CLR
1040 PRINT "YOU BEAT THE DEVIL"
1050 PAUSE 250
1060 CLR
1070 PRINT "CARE TO TRY AGAIN?"
1080 PRINT "TYPE Y OR N."
1090 IF INKEY$ = "Y" THEN GOTO
290
1100 If INKEY$ <> "Y" THEN GOTO
1110
1110 IF INKEY$ = "N" THEN GOTO
1200
1120 IF INKEY$ <> "N" THEN GOTO
1090
1200 CLR
1210 PRINT "THANKS FOR A DEVIL-
ISHLY"
1215 PRINT "GOOD GAME."
```

```
1220 PRINT "HOPE WE CAN PLAY"
1225 PRINT "AGAIN SOON."
```

Somehow that pun in line 1210 doesn't stink quite so badly when you see it printed out on a computer screen.

```
2000 CLR
2010 PRINT "OOPS -- HIT A LINE."
2020 PRINT "START OVER."
2030 PAUSE 300
2040 GOTO 290
```

Lines 2000 through 2040 carry out the penalty for bumping into the maze.

Notice something missing from this program? Right: a scoring device. You have the job of supplying that. Look at how we scored previous games, then work out a system for scoring this one.

You can tinker with the program in other ways, too. Do you really think it's fair to make a player start all over for bumping into the maze? Maybe a lesser penalty, such as a ten-point loss, would suffice. It's up to you!

Finally, those four old plain horizontal lines are a poor excuse for a maze. Undoubtedly you can do better. How would you print out a more complex maze? And how would you program the computer to register when the player has bumped into a maze wall?

That could make the program a little complicated, but it might be fun!

Now for a maze-type game with a more sophisticated scoring system.

CHAPTER 8

Tiger's Run

SOONER OR LATER, all students of computer game design run into the word "algorithm." It isn't the name of a 1920s dance, or of a legendary baseball manager. An algorithm is a mathematical concept that might be described as the best possible way of doing something.

Although you may never have heard of them before, algorithms play important roles in many things we do, from fighting wars to controlling traffic flow at intersections. Algorithms help to speed air travelers on their way and keep down grocery prices at the supermarket. In short, a lot of things would be very difficult if not impossible to do without algorithms.

A classic introduction to algorithms is the famous problem of the traveling salesman. A salesman has to make a business trip from New York to San Francisco. He has only so many days for the journey and can make only a certain number of stops. What route should he take, stopping at which cities, to maximize his sales?

If this problem sounds easy to you, then try it yourself. You will find that high-school algebra isn't much help!

Working out the most profitable route for the salesman is so complicated that you may have to rely on trial and error more than on anything else in your search for the answer.

Naturally, using trial and error is a very wasteful and time-consuming procedure. So mathematicians have devoted a lot of time and effort to more effective ways of finding useful algorithms. We won't go into their methods here, but we ought to talk briefly about algorithms as they bear on computer game design.

Many popular computer games require players to work out algorithms. Suppose you are fighting a space battle on screen, and the computer keeps throwing several different kinds of alien spacecraft at you. On which kind should you concentrate your fire to make the highest possible score?

That's an example of a search for an algorithm. Call it an optimum avenue of play, if you like.

Virtually all game play can be seen as a quest for better and better algorithms, because players want to win, and the player with the most effective algorithm is likely to be the winner.

So the next time you turn on the TV and see the Monsters trying to rip apart the Behemoths on a gridiron somewhere, what you're watching isn't merely a bone-jarring display of contact sport. It's also a search for a winning algorithm! (Tell that to the coach sometime.)

Here is a game that was set up with algorithms in mind.

Tiger the cat has a problem. He has escaped from his owner's car on a trip to the vet and is about a mile from home. Between Tiger and his house lie several fields of grass and brush, each with a different concentration of fleas. As Tiger passes through those fields, fleas will hop onto him.

Tiger's goal is to get home with the minimum possible number of fleas. Which route should he take?

The answer isn't easy to find, because of how the flea densities are arranged. Look at the following map:

```
1111222223333334444444444555550 . . . Finish
1111222223333334444444444555555
1111222223333334444444444555555
```

```
1111222223333334444444444555555
1111222223333334444444444555555
1111222223333334444444444444444
1111222223333334444444444444444
1111222223333333333333333333333
1111222223333333333333333333333
1111222223333334444444444444444
1111222223333334444444444444444
1111222223333334444444444444444
1111222223333333333333333333333
1111222223333333333333333333333
1111222222222222222222223333333
1111222222222222222222223333333
1111222222222222222222223333333
1111222222222222222222223333333
1111111111111111222222223333333
1111111111111111222222222222222
Start . . . x1111111111111111222222222222222
```

Tiger will start out at the lower left and work his way upward to his home at the upper right. Here Tiger is symbolized by an X and his home by a 0, just as in the Jersey Devil game.

Zone 1 has the lowest density of fleas. With each step Tiger picks up only one additional flea. The density increases by one flea per step with each successive zone, up to five.

The zones are positioned so that Tiger cannot avoid the high-density areas. He can attempt to compensate by spending as much time as possible in the relatively flealess areas, saving up for a dash across the flea-rich zones.

Yet Tiger cannot tarry too long in the low-density areas, because a long march through them, picking up one flea per step, might actually leave him more flea-ridden than a relatively fast passage through the high-density parts of the map!

Which route will give Tiger the fewest fleas? You'll have to work that out for yourself—and hope that Tiger doesn't get too sick of flea powder before you're done.

The first part of the program will print out the maze. Note how GOSUB . . . RETURN loops are used to save time and effort:

```
05 REM "FLEAS"
09 CLR
```

```
10 PRINT "111122222333333444444444555550"
20 GOSUB 50
30 GOSUB 50
40 GOSUB 50
50 PRINT "111122222333333444444444555555"
55 RETURN
60 GOSUB 70
70 PRINT "111122222333333444444444444444"
75 RETURN
80 GOSUB 90
90 PRINT "111122222333333333333333333333"
95 RETURN
100 GOSUB 120
110 GOSUB 120
120 PRINT "111122222333333444444444444444"
125 RETURN
130 GOSUB 90
140 GOSUB 90
150 GOSUB 170
160 GOSUB 170
170 PRINT "111122222222222222222223333333"
175 RETURN
180 PRINT "111111111111222222222223333333"
190 GOSUB 200
200 PRINT "111111111111222222222222222222"
210 PRINT
```

Now we're through with the maze-printing part of the program. See how much labor the GOSUB . . . RETURN loops saved you? Whenever one line is identical to another, you need only type out that line's pattern once and put it in a GOSUB . . . RETURN loop to be duplicated whenever necessary. Without that time- and labor-saving device, you probably still would be typing out long strings of numbers right now.

Having set up the field of play, we're now ready to see what makes Tiger run.

```
210 C = 0
```

Line 210 signifies that Tiger starts his run in a flealess condition. Variable C stands for how many fleas he's picked up.

```
220 A = 20
230 B = 1
```

These are Tiger's initial coordinates, which place him at the lower left corner of the maze.

```
240 PRINT AT A,B; "X"
```

And there's Tiger himself, raring to go.

The next few lines should look familiar to you. They're almost identical to the ones we used to move our nervous traveler through the swamp in the Jersey Devil game.

This time, however, there's no "track covering" involved, because we want Tiger's trail to show up on the screen. One of your goals here is to find the route that takes Tiger home with the fewest fleas on him, and for that you will have to see his routes printed out. Then you can match his path on each individual run with the number of fleas accumulated and see how well your algorithm worked out.

```
250 D$ = INKEY$
260 IF D$ = "" THEN GOTO 250
270 IF D$ = "L" THEN B = B - 1
280 IF D$ = "R" THEN B = B + 1
290 IF D$ = "U" THEN A = A + 1
300 IF D$ = "D" THEN A = A - 1
```

If you can't figure out what's going on in lines 400 through 500, you just haven't been paying attention!

```
400 IF A = 1 THEN GOTO 1000
410 IF A = 2 THEN GOTO 1100
420 IF A = 3 THEN GOTO 1200
430 IF A = 4 THEN GOTO 1300
440 IF A = 5 THEN GOTO 1400
450 IF A = 6 THEN GOTO 1500
460 IF A = 7 THEN GOTO 1600
470 IF A = 8 THEN GOTO 1700
480 IF A = 9 THEN GOTO 1800
490 IF A = 10 THEN GOTO 1900
500 IF A = 11 THEN GOTO 2000
510 IF A = 12 THEN GOTO 2100
520 IF A = 13 THEN GOTO 2200
530 IF A = 14 THEN GOTO 2300
540 IF A = 15 THEN GOTO 2400
550 IF A = 16 THEN GOTO 2500
560 IF A = 17 THEN GOTO 2600
570 IF A = 18 THEN GOTO 2700
580 IF A = 19 THEN GOTO 2800
590 IF A = 20 THEN GOTO 2900
```

As you probably saw, lines 400 through 590 are part of the "tracking" program that keeps the computer informed of where Tiger is. If he is at A coordinate so-and-so, the program tells the computer to check his B coordinate too and figure out which zone of flea density the cat is passing through.

Note the logic of these lines. If the computer were thinking in plain English, then it would be saying to itself something like this:

"Let's see: If Tiger isn't at the upper end of the line, then he must he somewhere toward the lower end; and if he isn't in the next lower section, then maybe he's in the next lower one beyond that." And so on, to the end of the line if necessary.

Eventually Tiger is located and, depending on which segment of the line (that is, which zone of flea density) he occupies, the computer goes on to a later section of the program and tacks another few fleas on Tiger's hide.

```
1000 IF B = 30 THEN GOTO 3000
1010 IF B < 30 THEN GOTO 1015
1015 IF B >= 25 THEN GOSUB 3100
1020 IF B < 25 THEN GOTO 1025
1025 IF B >= 15 THEN GOSUB 3200
1030 IF B < 15 THEN GOTO 1035
1035 IF B >= 10 THEN GOSUB 3300
1040 IF B < 10 THEN GOTO 1045
1045 IF B >= 5 THEN GOSUB 3400
1050 IF B < 5 THEN GOSUB 3400
1060 GOTO 240
```

"Whoa!" you may say at this point. "Why is the number 3000, in line 1000, preceded by GOTO, while all the other 3000-range numbers in the rest of this program block are preceded by GOSUB?"

Good question—it shows you're noticing the little but important details in game programs.

Look back at line 400. If A equals 1, it says, then jump ahead to line 1000. If Tiger has finally arrived home, then B will equal 30 (since 1, 30 are the home coordinates). In that case there's no need for GOSUB . . . RETURN loops to keep him hopping through the fields, and line 1000 will refer you to the last stretch of the program, where the computer will tell you how well Tiger fared on this run.

Before you go any farther, better go through lines 1000 through 1060 once again to make sure you understand the scoring procedure here.

The GOSUB . . . RETURN loops are about to come in handy once again. In the next few lines of the program they will save you from having to write out the same set of commands again and again.

```
1100 GOSUB 1400
1200 GOSUB 1400
1300 GOSUB 1400
```

Why are lines 1100 through 1300 alike? Because the topmost three lines of the diagram are identical and therefore scored in the same way.

```
1400 IF B <= 30 THEN GOTO 1405
1405 IF B >= 25 THEN GOSUB 3100
1410 IF B < 25 THEN GOTO 1415
1415 IF B >= 15 THEN GOSUB 3200
1420 IF B < 15 THEN GOTO 1425
1425 IF B >= 10 THEN GOSUB 3300
1430 IF B < 10 THEN GOTO 1435
1435 IF B >= 5 THEN GOSUB 3400
1440 IF B < 5 THEN GOSUB 3500
1450 RETURN
```

Relax; from here on it gets easier.

```
1500 GOSUB 1600
1600 IF B <= 30 THEN GOTO 1605
1605 IF B >= 15 THEN GOSUB 3200
1610 IF B < 15 THEN GOTO 1615
1615 IF B >= 10 THEN GOSUB 3300
```

```
1620 IF B < 10 THEN GOTO 1625
1625 IF B >= 5 THEN GOSUB 3400
1630 IF B < 5 THEN GOSUB 3500
1640 RETURN
1700 GOSUB 1800
1800 IF B <= 30 THEN GOTO 1805
1805 IF B >= 15 THEN GOSUB 3200
1810 IF B < 15 THEN GOTO 1815
1815 IF B >= 10 THEN GOSUB 3300
1820 IF B < 10 THEN GOTO 1825
1825 IF B >= 5 THEN GOSUB 3400
1830 IF B < 5 THEN GOSUB 3500
1840 RETURN
1900 GOSUB 1600
2000 GOSUB 1600
2100 GOSUB 1600
```

Why GOSUB 1600? Simple. These three lines of the diagram are printed out and scored identically with the seventh and eighth lines from the top, so we can go back and use them instead of writing out all that stuff over again.

```
2200 GOSUB 1800
2300 GOSUB 1800
2400 GOSUB 2600
2500 GOSUB 2600
2600 IF B <= 30 THEN GOTO 2605
2605 IF B >= 25 THEN GOSUB 3300
2610 IF B < 25 THEN GOTO 2615
2615 IF B >= 5 THEN GOSUB 3400
2620 IF B < 5 THEN GOSUB 3500
```

```
2625 RETURN
2700 IF B <= 30 THEN GOTO 2705
2705 IF B >= 25 THEN GOSUB 3300
2710 IF B < 25 THEN GOTO 2715
2715 IF B >= 15 THEN GOSUB 3400
2720 IF B < 15 THEN GOSUB 3500
2725 RETURN
2800 GOSUB 2900
2900 IF B <= 30 THEN GOTO 2905
2905 IF B >= 10 THEN GOSUB 3400
2910 IF B < 10 THEN GOSUB 3500
2915 RETURN
```

Now we're ready for the part of the program that tacks the fleas on Tiger and ultimately announces his arrival.

```
3000 CLR
3010 PRINT "YOU MADE IT"
3020 PRINT
3030 PRINT "TOTAL FLEAS ACCUMULATED:
"; C
3035 PRINT
3040 PRINT "CARE TO TRY AGAIN?"
3050 PRINT
3060 PRINT "(TYPE Y OR N.)"
3070 E$ = INKEY$
3080 IF E$ = "" THEN GOTO 3070
3085 IF E$ = "Y" THEN GOTO 09
3090 IF E$ <> "Y" THEN GOTO 3091
3091 IF E$ = "N" THEN STOP
```

```
3092 IF E$ <> "N" THEN GOTO 3070
3100 C = C + 5
3110 RETURN
```

Tiger accumulates five fleas there . . .

```
3200 C = C + 4
3210 RETURN
```

. . . four fleas there . . .

```
3300 C = C + 3
3310 RETURN
```

. . . and so on.

```
3400 C = C + 2
3410 RETURN
3500 C = C + 1
3510 RETURN
```

That's it for now. You are free to carry the program farther if you wish.

A lot of rough edges were left on this program so you could smooth them down for practice. For example, you can easily eliminate some of those GOSUB . . . RETURN loops and thus make the program much shorter and cleaner. If you haven't already seen how to do so, then a quick review of the program ought to reveal the method to you. Just bear in mind how easily a GOSUB . . . RETURN loop allows you to duplicate things.

You can also arrange for the computer to remember all your scores and to print them out on the screen when requested, to show how you are progressing in your search for the best algorithm.

You can even program the computer to announce, at the end of a game, whether you have come up with a better algorithm—that is, beaten your best previous score.

CHAPTER 9

Stringing Along

COMPUTERS HAVE a reputation for being mere "number crunchers," unable to handle anything except numbers and a very few words such as GOTO, RETURN, and so forth.

Yet computers are more versatile than that. They can recognize words, phrases, and even whole sentences if you know how to write an appropriate program.

To do that, you can use "string functions." They are similar to INKEY\$, which you used in the casino game several chapters back.

INKEY\$ allowed you to enter a letter, such as Y or N, instead of a number. String functions go a little farther. They allow you to designate a whole string of letters—a word, a sentence, or whatever—by a letter followed by a dollar sign. Here are some examples:

```
A$ = "VERMONT"
A$ = "1234567890"
A$ = "#%&?!!!!"
```

Strings like that last one come in handy sometimes, as one well-known figure in arcade games can tell you.

The letters or numbers or whatever in the string *must* be enclosed in quotes as we've just shown or the computer won't recognize them as a string.

This is how a computer, though designed to work mainly with numbers, also can handle words. Let's try a simple program to show how string functions may work in a game.

The computer starts by putting a riddle to you:

```
10 PRINT "SOFT AS VELVET,"
20 PRINT "SHARP AS KNIVES,"
30 PRINT "THIS CREATURE HAS"
40 PRINT "EIGHT PLUS ONE LIVES."
```

Eight plus one is nine, so the answer must be "cat." Here's how we get the computer to recognize that word:

```
50 A$ = "CAT"
60 INPUT B$
```

Here B$ is your written answer to the riddle. Just type in "CAT" and hit the RETURN key.

```
70 IF A$ = B$ THEN GOTO 100
```

If you type in the correct answer, then A$ will equal B$, and the computer will proceed to line 100 and inform you that you are correct. But if you choose the wrong answer, or if you make an error and type in CAY or CAR instead of CAT, then:

```
80 IF A$ <> B$ THEN GOTO 200
```

Line 80 will send you along to line 200, which tells you to try again.

```
100 PRINT "THAT'S RIGHT."
110 STOP
200 PRINT "SORRY, WRONG ANSWER."
```

Be sure that STOP is inserted in line 110. Otherwise the computer will continue after line 100 and print out two contradictory responses:

```
THAT'S RIGHT.
SORRY, WRONG ANSWER.
```

That STOP keeps the computer (and the player) from getting confused.

Here's another easy program to get you accustomed to using string functions. This time you have to guess a word with only a few letters for clues.

```
10 PRINT "I AM THINKING OF AN EIGHT-
"
20 PRINT "LETTER WORD. IT IS SOME-
THING"
30 PRINT "YOU SEE AT HOME EVERY DAY."
40 PRINT
50 PRINT "I WILL GIVE YOU ONE LET-
TER"
60 PRINT "AT A TIME, AND YOU MUST
GUESS"
70 PRINT "THE WORD. YOU WILL HAVE
THREE"
80 PRINT "GUESSES. IF YOU GUESS COR-
RECTLY,"
90 PRINT "YOU WIN. IF YOU DO NOT
GUESS THE"
100 PRINT "CORRECT ANSWER WITHIN
THREE"
110 PRINT "ATTEMPTS, YOU LOSE."
120 PRINT "READY? GOOD LUCK."
125 A$ = "COMPUTER"
```

The word "computer" isn't printed out on the screen at this point, of course. It's a secret between you and the computer.

126 A = 0

Remember our old friend the A variable? This time it's back for much the same job it performed in the Russian roulette game. The A variable will make sure you get *only* three guesses.

Just don't get A confused with A$! That dollar sign means that A$ literally has strings attached.

```
130 PRINT
140 PRINT "HERE IS YOUR FIRST CLUE:"
150 PRINT
160 PRINT "_ _ _ _ _ T _ _"
170 PRINT
180 GOSUB 1000
```

This is all straightforward. Lines 130 through 170 provide your first clue, which in this case is the fifth letter of the unknown word. Then line 180 refers the computer to a subroutine that determines whether you guessed the right answer.

```
185 IF A < 3 THEN GOTO 200
190 IF A = 3 THEN GOTO 3000
```

Here the A variable pops up again. If you have used up all three of your tries, then A will equal 3, and line 190 will send you along to line 3000, which tells the correct answer.

If you have another two turns coming, however, then A will be less than 3, and line 185 will whisk you along to line 200 for another try:

```
200 PRINT "HERE IS YOUR SECOND CLUE:"
210 PRINT
```

```
220 PRINT "C _ _ _ _ T _ _"
230 GOSUB 1000
```

Here we go again.

```
240 IF A < 3 THEN GOTO 300
250 IF A = 3 THEN GOTO 3000
```

One more chance. Better put on your thinking cap.

```
300 PRINT "HERE IS YOUR THIRD CLUE:"
310 PRINT "C _ M _ _ T _ _"
320 GOSUB 1000
330 GOTO 3000
```

Line 330 is there just in case you guess wrong on all three tries. It refers the computer to a little condolence message for losing players.

```
1000 PRINT "IF YOU THINK YOU HAVE"
1010 PRINT "THE ANSWER, TYPE IT IN."
```

Go ahead. Type in something. You might be right!

```
1020 INPUT B$
1030 IF B$ = A$ THEN GOTO 2000
```

If you're really smart and guess correctly on the first attempt, then line 1030 sends you down to the victory announcement in line 2000.

```
1040 IF B$ <> A$ THEN GOTO 1050
```

If you don't guess it right the first time, don't get too upset. Lines 1040 through 1070 give you another chance!

$$1050 \quad A = A + 1$$

Each time you go through this GOSUB . . . RETURN loop without guessing the correct answer, that equation in line 1060 adds one to the value of A, thus telling the computer how many tries you've made.

```
1060 PRINT "SORRY. TRY AGAIN."
1070 RETURN
2000 PRINT "CORRECT. THE WORD IS
'COMPUTER.'"
2010 STOP
3000 PRINT "SORRY. THE WORD WAS
'COMPUTER.'"
```

Again, don't forget the STOP in line 2010.

Here's a variation on the same kind of game. It's called a "substitution cipher" and merely replaces one letter of the alphabet with another in a sentence. Below, for example, is a famous quotation rewritten in a partial substitution code:

MZPEH JAXVS.

Some of the letters remain the same as in the original quote, but some are changed. Your job is to figure out which are changed, which are not, and what the original saying was.

Looks vaguely familiar, doesn't it? Some bit of ancient wisdom, perhaps?

In the following game, the player gets five chances to guess the original quotation.

```
10 PRINT "HERE IS A WELL-KNOWN SAY-
ING"
20 PRINT "CONCEALED IN A PARTIAL"
30 PRINT "SUBSTITUTION CODE."
```

```
35 PRINT "THE FIRST AND LAST LETTERS
OF THE
40 PRINT "QUOTE ARE UNCHANGED  OTHER
LETTERS"
45 PRINT "MAY BE ALTERED."
46 PRINT
50 PRINT "   MZPEH JAXVS."
60 PRINT
70 PRINT "YOU WILL HAVE FIVE CHANCES"
80 PRINT "TO  GUESS  THE  ORIGINAL
QUOTE."
90 A = 5
95 A$ = "MONEY TALKS"
```

That's *very* ancient wisdom.

```
100 GOSUB 200
110 GOSUB 200
120 GOSUB 200
130 GOSUB 200
140 GOSUB 200
200 PRINT "WHAT'S YOUR GUESS?"
210 INPUT B$
```

Here you type in whatever you think the right answer is.

```
220 IF B$ = A$ THEN GOTO 300
230 IF B$ <> A$ THEN A = A - 1
240 PRINT "SORRY ... TRY AGAIN."
250 PRINT "YOU HAVE "; A ; " GUESSES
LEFT."
260 IF A > 0 THEN RETURN
270 IF A = 0 THEN GOTO 400
```

```
300 PRINT "ABSOLUTELY RIGHT,"
310 PRINT "O FOUNT OF KNOWLEDGE."
320 STOP
400 PRINT "SORRY. THE ANSWER WAS:"
410 PRINT
420 PRINT "   MONEY TALKS."
```

See how easily computers can handle words when you know how to program them in? These exercises ought to give you ideas for more sophisticated word-game programs.

CHAPTER 10

Up
and Over

It's TIME to put more action into our games. So let's simulate a lively athletic event—the pole vault. This will provide an opportunity to explore making graphics further and to introduce a function that will serve you well in games you may design.

You've seen a pole vault many times, either at athletic meets or on TV. The pole-vaulter gets a running start, plants the pole in the ground just before reaching the crossbar and supports, and uses the pole to lift himself or herself up and—if the pole-vaulter is lucky—over the crossbar. This is one of those games where you either win or lose, for anyone can see whether the athlete has cleared the bar.

But how can we simulate the high-flying curve of the pole-vaulter's flight through the air? For this we will have to call on the SIN function.

SIN has nothing to do with morality. It's the "sine function." If you have taken trigonometry in school, you have seen a sine curve drawn on the board. It's a neat, symmetrical curve that looks like this:

This is what is known as a "pure" sine-wave function, un-complicated by any other factors. We can put SIN to good use in our pole-vault simulation by converting that undulating, snaky motion into a "parabola" like the one on page 103.

This is roughly the trajectory that our pole-vaulter will follow. Think of it as a "slice" of a sine curve.

READ YOUR SYSTEM'S PROGRAMMING MANUAL BEFORE GOING FURTHER

Wise words. If you didn't bother to study your system's programming manual carefully before trying the exercises in this book, chances are you've been having trouble. Now that we are getting into reasonably complicated games, it is more important than ever before that you familiarize yourself with your system's BASIC variant and how to convert these programs into it. If you are still asking yourself, "How do I get this thing to clear the screen?" then put this book down right now and spend tonight going over your system's manual.

The manual may be printed in type one micron high, and it may read as if written by an adding machine that was forced to eat a dictionary, but buckle down and master it anyway. (Look on the bright side: Maybe you can use the manual as proof that you've learned a "foreign" language!)

Ready? Let's get started.

We are about to see one reason why all that work with the manual is necessary. This game will require you to plot a curve on the screen, and there are many different ways to do it, depending on the nature of your system and the BASIC "dialect" it uses.

Some systems are straightforward. They let you use a one-word command such as PLOT or DRAW to turn an equation into a diagram.

Unfortunately, not all systems make things so easy for you. If you own one of the more sophisticated and intractable computers, you may have to perform all kinds of programming gymnastics to get a picture to appear on the screen.

In that sad event, you have everybody's sympathy. Sometimes one sees grown men and women reduced to mounds of blubbering jelly by the complex programming required to make some systems draw a simple little line or circle.

Luckily for you, programming need not drive you mad. You may be able to purchase or look up special programs that convert your system's BASIC into something slightly easier to use. Generally these programs are inexpensive, and some are available in back issues of computer magazines.

If you have the stamina of a mountain goat and the mathematical gifts of an M.A. candidate, you may even be able to conquer computer "machine language" (more about that a little later) and write your game programs solely in numbers, without even bothering to write in verbal commands and statements. If that day comes, you will be reknowned as a Bach of the bytes, a Paganini of programmers, and superstitious friends may start to wonder if perhaps, like Faust, you sold your soul for knowledge.

To save space here, we will use PLOT to produce a picture of the pole-vaulter's path through the air. The curve will be made up of points drawn at seventeen locations. And since the curve-generating equation will be the heart of our pole-vaulting program, let's put the equation somewhere in the middle of the program:

```
305 FOR N = 1 TO 17
310 B = SIN (N / 30 * PI)
```

Here B represents each vertical coordinate along the curve, and N stands for the horizontal coordinate. So the first coordinate (N,B) will be located at (1,B), or the far left-hand side of the screen. The high point of the jump will occur at about (9,B), and the athlete will return to earth at (17,B).

What about SIN (N / 30*PI)? Why not just tell the computer to print out SIN N?

That extra material in parentheses is there for a good reason.

It makes sure that the curve starts out on the ground—that is, at the lower left corner of the screen—rather than up in the air someplace.

But doesn't this equation still need something extra? Right. The equation has two big shortcomings.

As it stands now, the equation will generate a very shallow curve, because no sine value ever exceeds 1.0. So the curve must be heightened greatly. In other words, we will have to multiply B by some fairly large number (say, 35 to 40) if the jumps are to look impressive.

Moreover, the unmodified equation will produce the same curve every time. Therefore we must inject some variation into B—and for that we call on RND once more.

We want the athlete to pass *near* the crossbar on each jump but not necessarily *over* the bar. After all, no jumper succeeds on every try, and the game is more interesting and realistic if there's a possibility of hitting the bar and spoiling the jump. One-sixteenth inch can mean the difference between failure and victory.

So we need allow only a little vertical variation—that is, just a slight uncertainty about the maximum B value.

This is easily done with the right use of RND. Let's insert line 300 as follows:

```
300 A = INT (RND * 4) + 35
```

This A value will do two things: It will carry the pole-vaulter a decent distance above the ground, and it will vary his or her altitude from one try to another. (Note the 35 at the end of the line. That numerical value sets the minimum height for the trajectory. We'll talk more about that number and its duties in a moment.)

All we have to do, then, is plug the A value into line 310:

```
310 B = A * (SIN (N / 30 * PI))
```

Why the double parentheses? Because the whole shebang from the right-hand side of the old equation is supposed to be multiplied by A. The parentheses act as a "fence" to make A's job easier.

Now we have:

```
300 A = INT (RND * 4) + 35
305 FOR N = 1 TO 17
310 B = A * (SIN (N / 30 * PI))
```

The next step is to plot out the curve on the screen. For that task, two lines will suffice:

```
320 PLOT N, B
330 NEXT N
```

Once again, remember to include NEXT N. Otherwise the computer won't remember to count off all the horizontal coordinates, and you will get only a single dot printed in the lower left corner instead of a nice, smooth curve.

The result ought to look approximately like this:

The athlete may be sailing through the air now, but as yet he or she has nothing to sail over (or into, as the case may be). The next step is to draw the crossbar and supports, using the familiar old techniques we used to create the maze in the Jersey Devil game.

Lines 100 through 150 produce a pair of vertical supports (with a slight difference in their lengths, to simulate perspective):

```
100 FOR X = 2 TO 21
110 PRINT AT X, 5; "I"
120 NEXT X
130 FOR X = 3 TO 20
140 PRINT AT X, 9; "I"
150 NEXT X
```

Lines 160 through 180 draw the crossbar:

```
160 FOR Y = 6 TO 8
170 PRINT AT 4,Y; "*"
180 NEXT Y
```

While we're at it, we might as well print in some cushions for the athlete to land on:

```
190 FOR Y = 21 TO 31
200 PRINT AT 21, Y; "-"
205 NEXT Y
210 FOR Y = 22 TO 32
220 PRINT AT 20, Y; "-"
225 NEXT Y
230 FOR Y = 23 TO 33
240 PRINT AT 19, Y; "-"
245 NEXT Y
```

With line 300, of course, the "jump equations" start.

Now that we have the crossbar in place, how do we tell if the pole-vaulter hit it or cleared it?

Think back to the number 35 at the end of line 300. As we noted earlier, that number sets the minimum altitude for the pole-vaulter. So to give him or her the best possible odds, we ought to set the crossbar at altitude 35 + 1, or 36, because the RND∗4 will add at least one to the 35.

If the pole vaulter's maximum altitude equals 36, then, he or she has hit the bar and failed. Any value greater than 36, on the other hand, means success! Writing this out in program form, we get:

```
350 IF B <= 36 THEN GOTO 400
360 IF B > 36 THEN GOTO 500
```

Lines 400 and 500 refer you to announcements of victory or defeat. Compose them however you wish.

The playing field ought to look somewhat like this when printed on the screen:

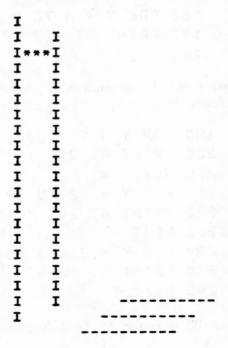

And with a trajectory plotted in:

```
        I
        I     I
          *.*I
        I     I
       .I     .
        I     I
     .  I        .
        I     I
   .    I     I     .
        I     I
        I     I
  .     I     I      .
        I     I
 .      I     I       .
        I     I
        I     I
.       I     I        .
        I     I
.       I     I       .
        I     I
.       I     I   ---.------
        I         ----------
              ----------
```

Now that you have the essential program worked out, try introducing some variations on it. For instance, a real pole-vault meet has several competitors. How about using INKEY$ to register any of three or four players? Then you can use the scoring techniques discussed in earlier chapters to tally up and display the scores in the upper right corner of the screen.

Also, it's possible to vary the height of the crossbar to provide low, medium, and high levels of challenge. That should be easy for you if you have mastered the GOSUB . . . RETURN loop. Just print out the bar at a different location, and alter lines 350 and 360 to reflect the change in height.

You can put in some interesting random variations if you wish. Here you have seen how to vary the height of a jump at random. Why not vary the length of a jump, too?

Suppose the meet is held in Chicago, and now and then a chance gust of wind off Lake Michigan sends a lightweight athlete sailing away on the breeze. How would you make that happen on screen? (Hint: Change the horizontal coordinates!)

You can put in fancier graphics if you feel up to designing them. Using GOSUB . . . RETURN loops, you can show the crossbar flying through the air after the vaulter hits it on an unlucky leap. You can even program a running figure to represent the athlete. Before you do so, however, you will need an introduction to advanced graphic design, and that will require a brief introduction to the sometimes tricky topic of machine-language programming.

Don't worry. It won't bite. But machine language is likely to baffle the novice programmer at first, so you had best have your system's programming manual at hand.

CHAPTER 11

POKEing Around

If you have played arcade games and watched those little stylized blobs of light flitting around the screen, you must have wondered what kind of programming makes them so fleet and agile—not to mention what gives them their shapes and colors, enables them to eat or shoot one another, and disintegrates them when they are shot or gobbled.

These games are the products of sophisticated programming involving "machine language"—the mathematical language in which computers "talk to themselves."

Machine language is not BASIC, or any other commonplace computer language you may be familiar with. BASIC is a language between plain English and the "native" language of the computer. For many of your purposes BASIC is adequate; but sometimes, to make the computer do complicated tasks, you will have to get down into machine language and talk to the computer, you might say, on its own level—in the numerical jargon of machine language.

You may have seen machine-language programs already. At first glance they look like arcane and incomprehensible muddles of weird words and numerals. Most frightening of all to a novice programmer and even to many experts are game programs written *entirely* in machine language, in this fashion:

```
50132: 089, 013, 167, 121, 167, 107,
045
50136: 167, 087, 169, 022, 033, 139,
187
50140: 026, 179, 023, 198, 056, 139,
179
```

And so on, for several pages. A sight like that can give even an experienced hacker the chills.

We won't get into that level of programming here. We will dip briefly into the techniques of advanced graphics programming, after which you will be free to plunge into your own system's programming manual and start making little figures dance across the screen.

The manual for your system ought to contain a "memory map" for the computer. This memory map is not a map like the kind you use on highway journeys. Rather, it lists the "addresses" of memory locations in your computer. Every memory location has a certain identifying number called its address, much as houses on a street have address numbers; and each memory location has its own specific job to handle, just as each addressee on a street is a person or a business in a particular line of work.

Confusing? Think of it this way: If you are sending a letter and you want it to reach the intended recipient, you have to put the recipient's address on the envelope: 45 Ward Street, for example. You must do much the same thing in advanced graphics programming. To make the program run as you want it to run, you will have to send messages (think of them as electronic "letters," if you like) to the appropriate locations, or addresses, in the computer's memory.

If you still have trouble understanding the concept of memory addresses, try visualizing them as numbers in a phone directory. Each number in the phone book corresponds to a specific person or family or business or whatever. To reach the party you want—say, Harry's Plumbing—you must first dial the right number: 555-5478, perhaps. Only then will Harry the plumber be able to help you.

This is pretty much what happens in machine language programming. To get what you want, you first have to "call" the right number. Here the phone book corresponds to the memory map.

Part of a highly simplified memory map might look like this:

```
ADDRESS          JOB

10 TO 1000       Screen memory
2000 TO 2100     Position animated
                 characters
10000 TO         Color animated
10100            characters
```

Please study the memory map for your system carefully, because it is the only way you will ever learn the "innermost thoughts" of your computer.

How do you tap into this mess of numbers? That is the job of POKE, the BASIC keyword that allows you access to the computer's memory, to do things such as designing and coloring your graphics and moving them around on the screen.

POKE is entered in a program as follows:

POKE A, B

Here A stands for the memory location, and B represents data to be POKEd into A. In everyday language, A is where the data are going, and B is the data to go in. POKE deserves its name, for it allows you to "poke," or insert, data into the memory at a given point.

If you were animating a cow on the screen, for example, and

wanted to color the cow purple, a typical computer might handle the coloring procedure this way:

POKE 12345, 6

Memory address 12345 handles coloring the cow, and data entry 6 tells the computer which color to use. Here the code number 6 stands for purple.

If you were giving the computer these instructions in everyday English, the conversation might go somewhat like this:

(Poke, poke. Telephone number 12345 rings. Computer answers.)

COMPUTER: Hello. Address 12345 here. Somebody want something painted some color?

YOU: Hey, 12345! Remember how to color a cow?

COMPUTER: Uh . . . yeah.

YOU: Well, here's a cow. Color it purple.

POKE enables you to do things that are difficult or impossible to do by other means. If you tried to animate a flying crossbar after looking through the pole-vault game earlier, you must have found it a sticky task indeed, even with GOSUB . . . RETURN loops to handle each step in the crossbar's flight. With POKE you could do it easily. We'll see how in a moment.

POKE also can make printing mazes much less difficult. Remember the rigamarole we went through to devise that maze in the Jersey Devil game? To print one single horizontal line of the maze, we had to go through a long string of operations. POKE would make the task easier.

Here is one way to do it:

```
10 FOR A = 1 TO 27
20 POKE A, ASC ("-")
30 NEXT A
```

That ASC deserves a bit of explanation, for you will find it handy as you proceed to higher and higher levels of game sophistication.

The ASC function (pronounced "ask") converts the hyphen between quotes into a special code called ASCII ("ask-ee"), which is short for American Standard Code for Information Interchange. ASCII represents all the letters of the alphabet and the numerals. Line 20 turns the hyphen into its equivalent ASCII code, which is then stored in the computer's memory. ASCII is the "interpreter," you might say, that helps translate familiar symbols—letters and numbers—into "language" the computer can deal with easily.

Let's examine the uses of POKE in greater detail and see how it can be used to translate a group of numbers in a program into a figure on a screen.

When you design a character in a game, you start with a good idea of what you want the character to be—an astronaut, a snake, a flying wombat, or whatever. So you have already decided what shape and color the character should have. Now your task is to convert your mental image of the character into something the computer can handle.

With POKE to help, that's not as hard as it might seem. A lot of the information needed to "construct" characters is built into your computer already. All you have to do is POKE the right memory locations, enter data to "draw" the characters, and POKE other memory locations to make the figures move around the way you wish.

By POKEing the various memory locations you can give the computer complete instructions for displaying your graphic creation, such as:

- How big the figure should be.
- What color or colors it should have.
- Where it should first appear on the screen.
- How fast and in which direction(s) it should move.

- What happens if the figure bumps into something else on the screen.

How you program these entries will, of course, depend on which system you are using. The machine language used in making these graphics will vary from one system to another. Even POKE isn't universally accepted; some systems use FILL instead. (Oh, the curse of Babel!)

POKE has a partner called PEEK. These two keywords are the Siamese twins of BASIC programming and commonly are mentioned together in the same breath, almost as a single expression. Computer programmers talk about "PEEK and POKE" the way music lovers talk about "Gilbert and Sullivan."

PEEK does just the opposite of POKE. PEEK takes things *out* of the computer's memory. Like POKE, PEEK has a descriptive name, for it provides a peek at what the memory holds. PEEK is written like this:

$$X = PEEK (Y)$$

Here X is a variable that you are setting to the value found at memory location Y. If you program in . . .

$$X = PEEK (1000)$$

. . . then X will take on the value of whatever is at memory address 1000.

A complete introduction to PEEK and POKE in game design is beyond the scope of this book, but the information you need is in the programming reference literature for your system. That literature should reveal how to use PEEK and POKE to hook up external controls—joysticks, paddles, and the like—for game play. These keywords also can be used on some systems to create music or sound effects to accompany the action on screen: a few bars of the "Hallelujah Chorus" to celebrate a winning score, or a screech and crash to enliven a highway accident. Again, check your manual for details.

Warning: You probably will find it difficult at first to think in terms of the machine language needed to use PEEK and POKE.

There will be times when you find yourself muttering something like, "Let's see . . . background color is determined by 23456 . . . or is it 34567? . . . No, that's to color in the dancing rhino . . . AAAAAAAARGH!!!"

The difficulty, however, is all in your mind. Machine language is hard to memorize only if you convince yourself that it's hard to memorize. And it's not, really.

You have probably committed lots of other, more complicated numbers to memory with no trouble, from your Social Security number to the phone numbers of your family and friends. Why should memory address numbers pose any greater problem?

Mastering memory address numbers is essentially no harder than memorizing a few phone numbers and area codes. Just work with the numbers a while and you should find them sticking in your memory automatically, so that memory address 23669 soon will seem as familiar as your own Zip Code.

Of course, the labor of typing in the numbers may get a little tedious at times; but if everything about game design were easy, then everyone would be designing games and there would be less opportunity for you to create a winner and make a bundle from it.

Luckily for you, many popular systems have special graphics-making programs that eliminate a lot of the POKEs and PEEKs by substituting other, easier-to-use programming. Ask your local computer dealer about these programs, or write to the company for details.

Game programmers often make a mistake that costs them a lot of wasted time and energy. They don't outline the action in their games clearly enough.

In an earlier chapter we outlined a game verbally, and that probably is enough as long as you are doing relatively simple games without much graphics content. When you start making hippos and snakes and jet fighters swoop and dance and slither around the screen, however, you will need a comprehensive visual guide to what is going on where and when.

Enter the storyboard.

The storyboard is a board on which the action of an animated game is outlined. On the board you will see several dozen index cards. Each card shows a particular scene, such as a jet shooting down a helicopter, or a glider pilot dodging a bloodthirsty flying wombat. The cards are arranged in sequence from the start of the game to the finish.

Animators use storyboards like this to make TV cartoons. Most of the familiar Saturday morning fare started out in storyboard form, because the storyboard is essential to an animated story. Since you will, in effect, be animating stories when you program arcade-style computer games, you ought to follow the example of professional animators and set up a storyboard for each game. Go down to the nearest office supply store and get a bulletin board—four feet by five feet is a convenient size—and mount it in your work area.

Then use ordinary index cards to outline the action in your game, step by step. Omit no dragon, elf, or battle cruiser. Make sure everything is there on the board, and you will be less likely to find yourself wondering, halfway through the game, what happened to those slimy green Gryzuks from Whott IV.

As we mentioned early in this book, arcade-style games may very well have peaked in popularity. They will be around for a long time to come, of course, just as pinball machines have lingered as a form of entertainment; but the arcade craze seems to be losing much of its initial momentum. (One quick but fairly reliable guide to the expected lifetime of a fad is its arrival on Saturday morning TV. When something shows up on a derivative kiddie show, then chances are its popularity is starting to slip.)

Rapidly growing in appeal (especially among well-to-do computer owners who have a lot of money to spend and therefore are a prime market for your work) is the "illustrated" story game, which offers the player both entertainment *and* an intellectual challenge—a combination that one seldom finds in arcade games. Making good story games is an art not easily taught, but the next chapter ought to give you some ideas to work on.

CHAPTER 12

The Plot
Thickens

"Tell me a story." That request keeps the entertainment industry in business. Everyone likes to hear a good yarn, whether it is told in a book, in a motion picture or TV show, on radio—or by a computer.

Each of these media has its strengths and weaknesses. For example:

- Books are inexpensive and pack lots of information into a very small space. A skilled storyteller can cram a whole world of excitement and adventure, wisdom and passion into a pocketful of printed pages and can conjure up in your imagination images that may delight you (or haunt your dreams) for the rest of your life.

  Dependence on print, however, creates problems for books. If the author is less than gifted at painting pictures with words, then the story probably will fall flat, and readers will find themselves holding two or three hundred gray pages of boredom. Unless just the right word is there on the page in front of you, the story will wither and die.

• A good radio drama can be just as evocative as a well-crafted novel, only here the spoken words and the sound effects stir the listener's imagination. In the right setting, the noise of coconut shells on a tabletop can become the approaching hoofbeats of the Grim Reaper's horse, and Casey's home run may be represented by a carrot breaking in half.

The trouble is that sound can suggest only so much and no more. Sometimes nothing but a picture—preferably a moving picture—can get an image across to the audience.

• Movies and TV are most colorful, as a rule, for they can show in dramatic visual images what books and radio have to convey through printed or spoken words, respectively. No mere verbal description quite captures the mood of the airport scene in *Casablanca* . . . or that interrupted dinner in *Alien* . . . or Jack Benny's befuddled stares. You have to see them directly to appreciate them, because they cannot be communicated adequately with words.

The problem with motion pictures and television is that they leave so *little* to the imagination. When you actually see the monster or the spaceship or whatever, the picture is unlikely to be even half as striking as the mental image you build up from a well-done book or radio drama. The most vivid images are those that exist *only* in the imagination—stirred up by a well-chosen word or sound that puts you in touch with your deepest fears or your dearest wishes. That's why film versions of popular stories so often fail at the box office: No picture on screen can ever match the images we create in our own minds. (It's also why many successful works of horror fiction never actually show or describe the villain or monster or whatever—or, if they do so, give us only the briefest glimpse of it. *Knowing* what the beast looks like would rob it of much of its terror.)

TV and film have another big limitation as well: They aren't "interactive." They offer the audience no chance to participate in the story. The tale is told there on the screen, and you either have to take it or leave it. You can't step into the narrative and tell Sam Spade what he's overlooking, or question Sherlock Holmes about his "deductive reasoning."

In fact, "interactive media" are few and far between. It's well nigh impossible to enter the story and participate in a novel, radio broadcast, or TV show. There have been a few experiments in audience and reader participation, using cable TV systems with push-button "response boxes" to record viewers' reactions, and books with multiple endings from which the reader is allowed to choose one. But such experiments are rare and have a mixed record of success and failure.

Ideally, the storytelling medium should combine the strong points of books, radio, TV, and movies and avoid most of their individual drawbacks.

Enter the computer.

A computer can display words before your eyes, just as a book does. It can show you pictures—not quite as detailed as those on the silver screen, but good enough to get the story across. And many home computers can produce sound effects, from the tiny tinkle of a symphony triangle to that visceral *splat!!* of a villain's body hitting the pavement after a well-deserved push from the fortieth floor.

How many other media can serve as a book, motion picture, and audio performance all rolled into one? Precious few. That's why computer entertainment seems to be moving away from videogames and in the direction of "story games"—tales that combine a printed-out text with graphics and sound effects.

Here's how a computer story game might run:

A picture appears on screen—the familiar orange span of the Golden Gate Bridge. Gray masses of fog drift slowly by as the title appears:

DEATH ON FRISCO BAY

From out of the mists rolls the lonely sound of a foghorn (which is easy to achieve if your computer has reasonably sophisticated sound-synthesis capabilities).

This will be a detective story. You, seated at the computer terminal, will try to solve the mystery—in this case, a murder mystery. And once the mystery is solved, you can go back and solve it again, for it is easy to program the game so it will have more than one possible solution.

MONDAY, APRIL 3. MY PHONE RANG AT 9:00 A.M. "HARTT AND CLUBB DETECTIVE AGENCY," I HEARD MY SECRETARY SAY.
MY SECRETARY'S NAME IS BERTHA. MY NAME IS CLUBB. SAM CLUBB. I TALK THIS WAY BECAUSE ONLY HALF OF MY MOUTH EVER MOVES. THE OTHER HALF IS FULL OF CIGARETTES.

The caller reveals there has been a murder. From there, the story can develop in any way you desire—or any combination of ways, for you may program the game to have several different outcomes, either chosen at random by RND or by the player, with the aid of string variables.

If you choose a random-selection process, you need only insert a line with RND, such as the following:

```
995 X = INT (RND * 3)
996 IF X = 1 THEN GOTO 1000
997 IF X = 2 THEN GOTO 2000
998 IF X = 3 THEN GOTO 3000
999 REM CHAPTER TWO STARTS HERE
```

Lines 1000, 2000, and 3000 open the three variants of the second chapter. The first might be set at Coit Tower, overlooking the bay; the second, in a restaurant in Chinatown; the third, at a storefront church in Oakland. In each case the characters, dialogue, and action are unique and send the narrative in a different direction.

Then, at the end of Chapter Two, another three possibilities appear . . . and so on, to the end of the story.

This kind of programming allows you to make literally dozens of stories out of your mystery. So every time the player tries to guess the outcome, he or she will be playing, in effect, a completely new game. Dozens of plays will occur before all the possible combinations are exhausted. (Note that you will have to keep the individual chapters brief so as not to exhaust the memory of your computer!)

Yet this is not, strictly speaking, an interactive game. A truly interactive game requires some active input from the player. Fortunately, such input is easy to arrange with the help of string functions. Here is how the first chapter might end:

```
SO NOW I HAD A CORPSE, A MEANS, AN
OPPORTUNITY ... AND ENOUGH SUSPECTS
TO FILL A TAXICAB.
    THE QUESTION WAS, WHICH OF THEM HAD
THE BEST MOTIVE TO COMMIT MURDER?
    WAS IT LITTLE FRENCHY, WHO LUSTED
FOR REVENGE?
    WAS IT FLO, THE JILTED LOVER?
    OR WAS IT THE MYSTERIOUS DR. FU,
ABOUT WHOM NO ONE SEEMED TO KNOW
ANYTHING CERTAIN?
```

That's the player's cue. Type in a name:

```
FLO
```

That input activates a line in the program:

```
IF A$ = "FLO" THEN GOTO 5000
```

Line 5000 initiates the following conversation:

```
"WELL, WHAT ABOUT IT, HONEY?" I
ASKED.
"THE STINKING RAT!" FLO SPAT OUT
THE WORDS LIKE BIG LEAD SLUGS FROM A
.38. "HE GOT WHAT WAS COMING TO HIM,
MR. CLUBB! LOOK AT THIS!"
SHE LIFTED UP HER GOLDEN TRESSES
WITH BOTH HANDS.
I THOUGHT I'D SEEN EVERYTHING IN
THIS BUSINESS, BUT WHAT I SAW . . .
```

You should have the idea by now. The player's entries—names, places, even simple yeses and noes—can guide the progress of the story. Each chapter is enlivened by graphics and sound effects. The result is an engaging combination of the printed word, video, and audio, with many possible outcomes.

How does this kind of game fit in with the guidelines we mentioned at the start of this book?

It has a goal—to discover the killer's identity.

It has rules—for example, you must base your deductions only on the evidence provided by the narrator.

It has a scoring system—if you guess correctly, you win. Otherwise, you lose.

It has a challenge—the intimidating task of sifting through all those clues.

Finally, it has the virtue of unpredictability—thanks to RND or string functions, whichever you choose to program in.

The story need not be a mystery, of course. It might just as well be a romance, science fiction, a Western, or any other genre. Whichever you select, bear in mind that this kind of computer game demands much more of you than a mere videogame. Here you have to excel in storytelling as well as in programming, and you must keep track of dozens of possible lines of plot development. That means you must design the game with a sharp eye on "continuity"—the entertainment industry's expression for making sure that everything in the story is compatible with everything else. So don't have a character strip down to his swim trunks and then, some minutes later, reach into his vest pocket to pull out an address book. To help avoid this kind of error you may have to generate a complicated storyboard that covers each possibility in detail, but the effort will pay off in smooth, continuous game play.

It's quite a job—but someone has to do it. And you'll get adept at juggling all the various elements (narrative, audio, and video) as time goes by.

So here's POKEing at you, kid.

CHAPTER 13

The "Thinking" Computer

ONE OF THE staples of science-fiction films is the intelligent computer. From the sinister HAL in Stanley Kubrick's film *2001* to the talking machines in George Lucas's movies, "thinking" computers have assumed major roles in the cinema and have given many viewers the idea that intelligent machines are just around the corner, if not here already.

Well, are they here already? Some people say yes, others no.

The subject of "artificial intelligence" (AI for short) has inspired a lot of debate in the scientific community, over the issue of whether a computer can be programmed to display intelligence as we understand it.

Since you are likely to hear much more about AI programs in years to come, you may be interested in exploring this branch of programming on your own—and maybe working some AI tricks into your games.

Much of the controversy over AI occurs because we really aren't sure what intelligence is. Like truth and justice and beauty, it's one of those things you can recognize but may have trouble explaining.

Just about every important philosopher in history has tried to figure out what intelligence is, and no one has come up with a satisfactory answer. So about forty years ago, a British mathematician named Alan Turing got fed up with the endless arguments over the nature of intelligence and suggested we stop trying to pin it down in a rigid definition.

Turing proposed instead a test for intelligence. It is now known as the "Turing test" in his honor and can be stated briefly:

```
IF WE RECOGNIZE CERTAIN BEHAVIOR AS
    INTELLIGENT, THEN IT REALLY IS
            INTELLIGENT.
```

Is this a good guide to intelligent behavior? You can decide for yourself after you have some experience writing AI programs.

Suppose you found a computer that could write poetry. That's intelligent behavior . . . or is it?

Before you make up your mind, meet GERTRUDE, a program devised a few years back as a simple example of AI programming. GERTRUDE writes verse. Not much of it is distinguished, but then, a computer writing verse is like Dr. Johnson's famous story of the dog walking on its hind legs: It may not be done well, but you wouldn't expect to see it done at all.

Here is a sample of GERTRUDE's "writing":

> Oh no, the birds left us.
> Will anyone cry?
> Don't ask me. . . . I know not. . . .
> And naught I espy.

You won't see any of GERTRUDE's verse in the *American Poetry Review*—but for a computer, her work isn't bad.

If you had looked at those lines without knowing their origin, would you have concluded that they came from a computer? Probably not. In all likelihood you would have figured that they were some child's effort to imitate Emily Dickinson.

In that case, GERTRUDE would pass the Turing test, for her behavior would be indistinguishable from that of an intelligent human being—namely, a poet (or would-be poet).

Is GERTRUDE therefore intelligent? You probably will say no when you see how the program is organized.

GERTRUDE's work is largely the result of RND operations and IF . . . THEN loops. RND selects numbers corresponding to several hundred different words and phrases in GER-TRUDE's vocabulary. The IF . . . THEN loops translate those numbers into words, which a single line near the end of the program arranges into a comprehensible order and displays on the computer screen.

GERTRUDE is too long a program to be written out in its entirety here, but a few small sections of it will serve to show how GERTRUDE was put together.

GERTRUDE starts as follows:

```
05 REM "GERTRUDE"
10 PRINT "HELLO. I AM GERTRUDE,"
20 PRINT "POET LAUREATE OF COMPUTER-
DOM."
30 PRINT "A COMPUTER IS A COMPUTER"
40 PRINT "IS A COMPUTER ... BUT SOME"
50 PRINT "COMPUTERS ARE MORE POETIC
THAN OTHERS."
60 PRINT
70 PRINT "STAND BACK--I FEEL INSPI-
RATION"
80 PRINT "COMING ON."
90 PRINT
100 A = INT (RND * 95)
101 GOSUB 200
102 B = INT (RND * 95)
103 GOSUB 300
```

```
104 C = INT (RND * 95)
105 GOSUB 400
```

Line 100 selects a number from 1 to 95. To see which word or phrase corresponds to that number, the computer follows the instruction in line 101 and "looks" down at line 200:

```
200 IF A = 1 THEN A$ = "A ROSE"
201 IF A = 2 THEN A$ = "THE SUN"
          • • •
299 RETURN
```

Here Gertrude is choosing the first word or couple of words in a line of verse (in most cases, the subject preceded by an article). Next comes the verb, which corresponds to a number selected by line 102 and is represented by the string B$:

```
300 IF B = 1 THEN B$ = "HAS"
          • • •
399 RETURN
```

And of course C$, which comes next, is the object of the sentence.

Finally, GERTRUDE lines up all the words in proper order and prints them out the screen:

```
1000 PRINT A$; B$; C$
```

This is a simplified account of GERTRUDE. Some special RNDs and GOSUB . . . RETURN loops were slipped in to handle asking questions, among other things.

Yet GERTRUDE was basically a very elementary program. It was long, but only because it required a fairly large vocabulary of English words. The operations in the program were within the understanding of a six-year-old; and once GERTRUDE's "inner secrets" are revealed, even small children can construct their own GERTRUDE-like programs.

GERTRUDE's apparent intelligence, then, is really nothing but "sleight-of-hand" programming. Does that mean *all* artificial intelligence programs are made up of similarly "dumb" programming that merely looks intelligent, much as a scarecrow looks like a living person when seen from a distance?

Maybe . . . or maybe not. A lot depends on your point of view.

From our viewpoint, the computer's "thinking" is absurdly simple when we see the program written out on paper—not much more than a group of character strings and IF . . . THEN loops.

But from a computer's viewpoint, our "sophisticated" thought patterns might not seem all that complicated, either. Much of our thinking consists of nothing more than IF . . . THEN. If you don't go to work, then you will stay home. If the car keys aren't in your pocket or purse, then they must be in the top bureau drawer. And so forth.

Maybe the human thinking "program" really is very similar to that of an AI-equipped computer . . . just more extensive. If that's the case, then an artifically intelligent computer might be intelligent by our standards, once it collected enough information.

Try devising some AI programs for yourself. They make good games—in fact, the *ultimate* compu.er games.

The goal here is to devise an intelligent computer program.

The rules are the conditions of the Turing test: Your program must convince a human user that the program really is intelligent.

Score the game play by the number of successful runs. If your program convinces users of its intelligence more than, say, seventy-five times out of a hundred, then you have a pretty good program.

There's plenty of challenge in a game like this. There's plenty of surprise, too, for as your program gets longer and more complex, it also will start acting less and less predictably. You may find the program doing things you never anticipated it would or could do, much as an intelligent human may surprise you with his or her behavior sometimes.

Don't be discouraged if your early efforts end in disappointment, for BASIC is not well suited to making AI programs. Trying to write an AI program in a rough-and-ready language like BASIC is somewhat like trying to write a Shakespearean sonnet in the shrieks, grunts, and gibbers of chimpanzee talk. For good AI programs you will need more sophisticated and versatile programming languages such as LISP, but BASIC will get you started.

Some researchers think we will never have truly intelligent computer programs. Other, more optimistic scientists and programmers think the development of such programs is just a matter of time.

Who knows? Maybe one of *your* programs will be the one that lifts computers above the level of mere unthinking machines and into the realm of intelligent, sentient beings. *Then* think of the games that humans and computers will be able to play with one another!

GAME DESIGN CHECKLIST

1. Have you avoided TOCs (tired old clichés)?
2. Does your game have a clearly defined goal?
3. Does the game have easily understandable but not too many rules?
4. Is there a definite scoring procedure? If the game is not scored numerically, is it clear who wins and who loses?
5. Does the game challenge the player?
6. Is there an element of unpredictability in your game?
7. Is the game thoroughly debugged?

If the answers to all these questions are yes, then you did your job well. Congratulations, and best of luck!

RECOMMENDED READINGS

Readers who want to learn more about computer game design may refer to dozens of magazines and books. Computer magazines come and go—at last count there were well over a hundred of them on the stands, with several "births" and "deaths" each month—so here are some of the most enduring and widely available publications of interest to game designers:

A+: The Independent Guide for Apple Computing. 1 Park Avenue, New York, NY 10016. A+ is colorful and full of practical suggestions for operating your computer and for designing games on it.

Ahoy! 45 West 34th Street, Room 407, New York, NY 10001. Intended for Commodore Users, *Ahoy!* contains many useful features, including game programs.

Compute! 505 Edwards Drive, Greensboro NC 27409. One of the biggest and slickest computer magazines, *Compute!* is one of the most informative as well. The game printouts are invaluable learning aids.

Compute!'s Gazette. 505 Edwards Drive, Greensboro, NC 27409. This lively offshoot of *Compute!* is aimed specifically at Commodore users and is especially helpful to novice programmers.

Creative Computing. 39 East Hanover Avenue, Morris Plains, NJ 07950. Valuable for its reviews of game-related hardware and software.

PC. 1 Park Avenue, New York NY 10016. Though it is intended primarily for IBM PC users, *PC* can teach readers much about game design and programming for almost any system.

Personal Computing. 50 Essex Street, Rochester Park, NJ 07662. Slick and colorful, *Personal Computing* is full of helpful advice for both the novice programmer and more advanced students.

Besides the operating and programming manuals for your particular system, here are some books you ought to have:

Bates, William *The Computer Cookbook: How to Create Small Computer Systems That Work for You.* Englewood Cliffs, N.J.: Prentice-Hall, 1983. A classic of home computer literature. *The Computer Cookbook* contains much valuable advice about game hardware and software.

Cowan, L. *The Illustrated Computer Dictionary and Handbook.* New York: Enrich/Ohaus. Well-illustrated and comprehensive, Cowan's book will help you make sense of the more opaque passages in computer documentation.

Lien, David. *The BASIC Handbook.* New York: CompuSoft Publishing, 1981. Lien's book is worth its weight in pure iridium, for it cross-references all the BASIC variants now on the market and will make it much easier for you to translate programs from one BASIC dialect into another.

Waite, Mitchell and Michael Pardee. *Basic Programming Primer*. Indianapolis, Ind.: Howard W. Sams & Company, 1982. Waite and Pardee provide clear explanations of BASIC programming techniques and include a few game programs as well as a handy "BASIC language reference card."

A QUICK BASIC GLOSSARY

Here, for quick reference, are most of the BASIC expressions used in this book. A more comprehensive list of BASIC terminology can be found in any BASIC programming manual, or in the manual for your particular computer system.

ASC

Converts a character in a string into a decimal ASCII code. For example:

```
10 IF ASC (A$) = 30 THEN STOP
```

FOR . . . NEXT

Carries out a loop with a variable in specified increments. The loop continues until the variable equals a maximum specified value. For example:

```
10 FOR X = 1 TO 10
20 PRINT X ** 3
30 NEXT X
```

GOSUB . . . RETURN

Refers to a subroutine starting with a line number listed after GOSUB, then refers back to the previous location in the program once the subroutine is finished. For example:

```
100 IF X = Y THEN GOSUB 200
200 PRINT "HOORAY"
210 RETURN
```

GOTO

Refers program execution to another line in the program, specified directly after GOTO. For example:

```
10 IF A = B THEN GOTO 100
```

IF . . . THEN

Allows action to continue if a certain condition is met. For example:

```
10 IF A = B THEN PRINT "IT WORKS"
```

INKEY$

A single-character string variable that allows the user to enter a character without subsequently hitting the RETURN key. For example:

```
100 LET Z$ = INKEY$
```

INPUT

Allows the user to enter values of variables; the RETURN key must be pressed after each entry. For example:

```
10 INPUT Q
```

PAUSE

Tells the computer to count from 1 to a number specified after PAUSE; used to pace action in games. May take many different forms depending on individual systems' BASIC variants. For example:

```
100 PAUSE 1 TO 100
```

PEEK

Sets a variable equal to a value found at a given memory location. For example:

```
100 X = PEEK (1500)
```

PLOT

Not common to all systems: transforms numerical data into specified printed patterns on the screen. For example:

```
100 FOR X = 1 TO 20
110 FOR Y = 5 TO 15
```

```
120 PLOT AT X, Y; "*"
130 NEXT X
140 NEXT Y
```

POKE

Allows entry of numerical data at a given memory location. For example:

```
100 POKE 12345, 4
```

PRINT

Displays given characters on the screen. For example:

```
10 PRINT "THIS IS A GAME"
```

RND

Random number selection function. For example:

```
10 LET X = INT (RND * 6)
```

STOP

Halts execution of a program. For example:

```
190 PRINT "THIS ENDS THE GAME."
200 STOP
```

TAB

Prints a specified number of empty spaces. For example:

```
10 PRINT TAB 5; "*"
```